LOOKING BACK AT

HOLIDAYS
1901 · 1939

Maggie Angeloglou

EP Publishing Limited 1975

This edition first published 1975
by EP Publishing Limited
East Ardsley, Wakefield, West Yorkshire,
England

ISBN: 0 7158 1121 5

Please address all enquiries to
EP Publishing Limited (address as above)

Text set in 11/12 pt. Photon Baskerville,
printed by photolithography, and bound
in Great Britain at The Pitman Press, Bath

LOOKING BACK AT
HOLIDAYS
1901 · 1939

Contents

S.O. 12-8

A MORN

RIDE ON THE SANDS, AT BLACKPOOL.

The town child on holiday. 1900–1914
"Just a song at twilight"

First of all, forget about go-away holidays. Most of you think of a holiday as being a week or so spent in a different place from your home — by the sea, or on a package deal trip abroad, and most of us can even imagine that two weeks in summer with an aunt in the country might be called a holiday, but when this story starts, over seventy years ago, very few people went away on holiday. They couldn't afford it.

Nowadays, workers have holiday pay which means that even if they are off work for a few weeks their pay packets are still filled, in fact they are supposed to have a few weeks' paid holiday which can be spread out over the year. That is apart from Christmas Day, Easter and the other bank holidays which may only be odd days but which are paid for all the same. At the beginning of this century a holiday off work meant no money, and it would often mean losing your job as well. So the fathers of families had no holidays and any mother who was working could not get away either.

But the children did not go away on their own, for many people were too poor to afford holidays. At that time there was a much greater difference between the rich and the poor. Rich children had holidays, poor children did not.

There were plenty of things to do when children were off school which were free or might cost very little. Any child who could manage to get about the streets on his own would wander for miles in the big cities and

On the beach. Buckets and spades at the ready.

also know his own area very well. In time he realised which fruit-stall owners might fling him some rotten oranges, or where he could snatch an illegal swim in the murky canals where barges still passed loaded with timber or coal. Poor children were used to walking in those days, and they were more able to look after themselves at an early age. Quite young boys and girls, often no older than ten, would be made responsible for all the little ones and were expected to take them away "out from under" their parents' feet. Homes were hardly places where these children

THE STALLS, HAMPSTEAD HEATH.
"FOOD AND DRINKS TO SUIT EVERY TASTE FOR ONE PENNY".

Edwardian Hampstead Bank Holiday. Food and drinks to suit every taste for one penny.

wanted to spend any time in those days, they were glad to have a chance to walk about aimlessly on every day of the school holiday, toting the babies on their backs in turn. In London the great place for holiday roamings was Hampstead Heath, and children would walk to it from the, then, grimy areas of Kentish Town or Camden Town, and spend the day paddling in its pools. It was more popular with poorer children than Kensington Gardens, the other haunt of boys and girls, possibly because Kensington was full of richer families with nannies who would frown on the ragged and often dirty children from the London slums. On Bank Holidays there was a fair on Hampstead Heath and parents would also manage to go to it. Some of the fairground machinery is still used today and you may be lucky enough to see it . . . usually merry-go-rounds with poles which are twisted like the golden barley sugar sticks which were also sold at fairgrounds, and with mechanical organs which sing out old popular songs — the songs our grandparents sang when they went home at last on warm, deep blue summer evenings, either walking or on a horsedrawn 'bus. The bus had

to wait for passengers at the bottom of the hill in Hampstead, because the hill was too steep for the horses to climb up!

Many of the fairground attractions have stayed the same . . . fortune tellers, doughnut makers, swinging gondolas, but now you will rarely see the pearly kings and queens who used to go to dance on Hampstead Heath at fairtime. They waltzed to the music of barrel organs, which were normally pushed. through the streets when there were no fairs. These barrel organs were shaped rather like small upright pianos, and were on two wheels with two shafts so that they could be lowered to the ground when the organ grinder wanted to play a tune. The bodies of the barrel organs were covered with paintings in gold leaf, or scarlet or blue and in every street they would bleat out "Goodbye Dolly Gray" or "Love's Old Sweet Song". But on holidays there would always be at least one barrel organ on the heath. People were more used to dancing outside in those days, especially in towns, and the arrival of a barrel organ or a German band would bring out all the young girls and men to waltz or jig in the gutters. There were few cars so the narrow lanes were very safe. A favourite tune to dance and sing to was "Ta-ra-ra-boom-de-ay" which was a popular music hall song. The pearly kings and queens dancing to it were an unusual sight which would make any child feel on holiday, for their clothes, which were normal enough in other ways, were sewn all over with tiny pearly buttons which twinkled as they moved. The men wore flat caps but the ladies had fashionable hats which were often three feet wide, with curled brims and drooping ostrich feathers which would wave in the air as they danced. Children who saw such sights, probably felt they had all the pleasures we would have from two weeks' holiday by the sea.

Nowadays it is rather sad to think of poor children wandering about in the streets because their homes are too small or too uncomfortable to stay in, but in the Edwardian age it was accepted that they only returned home when it was growing dark. However, a child who had walked in London from morning until night might have had more fun than we would think possible today. Most of the traffic was horsedrawn and a car was such a surprise that any boy would feel that his day was made if he had a chance to look at one close up. The were rather more like dragons than cars, with enormous carriage lantern eyes, lit in the dusk by paraffin flares, and long hooters like hunting horns, of gleaming brass, fixed by the driver's right hand. The bodies were often leather or basket covered, and the cars still caused a stir wherever they were driven. The other transport on the roads would make us stop and stare, but our grandparents would not have spared a second glance for hansom cabs, or elegant open carriages in which fashionable ladies drove about Hyde Park, or the milk traps which brought milk to the door in churns. Housewives and the servants (who seemed to make up half the population of London in those days) would run out with jugs which were filled from the churn with a tin measure, rather as we would buy paraffin for oil heaters today.

Children loved to stop and stare in those days and any hole in the road would have its

Skating and the art of balance.

collection of ragamuffins around it especially if they were off school. Street shows were free and often warming, for old men who roasted chestnuts might be persuaded to allow the children to stand near the brazier on cold days and would even give them a few chestnuts.

And in winter there were skaters. Either winters were much more cold or our grandparents were more daring, for as soon as ice had formed, a bevy of skaters would move onto it. "The Gentry" would wear special skating clothes, with sable or beaver muffs and hats, and warm gaiters, but poorer people ventured out on the ice too, only instead of shining skates imported from Germany which their companions wore to swoop about on the lake in St. James' Park, they would plough across the ice with blade bones on their feet, begged from a friendly butcher. Most grandparents remember using bones as skates, but nobody remembers if they were any use . . . we can imagine a lot of falls on the ice through skating on them.

A great many children from poor homes

11

never went to school if they could help it. Their parents saw no advantage in education, for you would have to be remarkably clever to escape from the mean streets and dead-ends jobs which most people were accustomed to thinking their only way of life. There were few chances to go on to any training unless you came from a very respectable, "comfortable" family. The children of clerks and small shopkeepers were privileged in those days, but the children of unskilled workers had very little chance to do anything better than their fathers and mothers, unless they joined the Army or Navy, and went "into service". Servants had safe, warm homes and a good life compared with a lot of their friends who had to fight to earn a little money as building workers or sewing women. So going to school often seemed fairly pointless. It didn't lead to anything and many of our great-grandparents, and grandparents too, only went to school occasionally and found jobs long before they were fourteen — the school leaving age — as shopboys, or baby minders, or helpers in the docks. Some of them did very well in spite of little schooling, but most of them must have wished when they were older that they had learned a little more.

In summer there was a very good reason to stop off school. Droves of families from the East End of London went hop picking.

This sounds like a treat, but it wasn't. It meant several weeks in the country, working in the fields and earning money. Hop pickers had lodgings found for them by the farmers for whom they worked and these were often great tents moored down on the fields or large barns where lots of families would camp out, protecting their privacy with old blankets hung as curtains across the room.

Most hop pickers would know each other; they would come from the same street, and they came year after year. There were three sorts of hop pickers: — the Londoners, who were very lively and noisy and who were thought rather vulgar in the villages; the country people who resented the invasion of the townspeople; and the gypsies who were liked by nobody and who were blamed for everything which went wrong from missing washing to bad weather. (Our grandparents were very superstitious, and gypsies had taken the place which witches once had in England.) These uneasy workmates picked hops in different parts of the fields, all distrusting each other.

Picking hops was not easy work. The hops are on tough vines which grow up poles and trellises. In summer they were sprayed with sulphur which came off on the pickers' hands, staining them and making them smell unpleasant. The mothers had the worst of it, for having brought down all their children they felt that they had to earn enough to justify the trip, and as children were bored with picking hops or ran away after a few minutes, they had to pick twice as fast to make up for their missing children. Often they had to keep an eye on the youngest child too, who would be laid out in a Moses basket or on an old coat, sleeping while his mother picked. The older children, who would have escaped to neighbouring fields and woods, were always in trouble with the farmers, and for very good reasons. In those days the ways of the country and the town were utterly different and town children might have been in a foreign country; they chased sheep, left gates open and ran onto crops. Their mothers' work was necessary for the Kent hop farmers but they must have often wished the children could have been left at home.

The villagers were very nervous of the noisy Londoners, and some small shops put wire netting in front of the counters so that the "invaders" couldn't handle the goods. Everybody was relieved when the impertinent, dirty children of the towns went back home.

There were other trips to the country. If a family had enough money they would go to Epsom for Derby Day, on the first Wednesday in June. This was a great holiday for townspeople and the costers would trot along in little donkey carts used for carrying vegetables or second-hand furniture at other times of the year. Spread out under the

The Pearly King and Queen, 1910. (Radio Times Hulton Picture Library.)

summer sun the turf at Epsom looked like a Bank Holiday scene with the same fortune tellers, the same barrel organs, the same chip fryers and the pearly clad dancers — some people looked at the race but most of them looked at each other.

Occasionally a street would organise a charabanc for the trip to Epsom and take along a cornet player who would root-a-toot his way onto the course. These big horse-drawn buses, filled with noisy cockneys, their cornets playing loudly in the sunlit lanes, were considered a great nuisance and finally they were banned . . . "The long serpentine line of costers' barrows and charabancs, played in by their cornettists, with, in between, the borrowed knifeboard 'bus. Then the long lines of hansom cabs with each driver

The Four-in-Hand leaving the Hotel Metropole at Brighton.

carrying a white favour cockily in his buttonhole, his topper shining or his white sporty 'bowler' cocked over one eye. Behind the hansom, again, the growler or four wheeler cab . . . And then, later in the morning, with the gypsies running by their sides, the victorias and barouches in which royalty and the nobility would arrive, with them the Four-in-Hands, driven by their gentlemen coachmen, turned out in spotless box-cloth and lemon-kid and wielding an exquisite lash with which they would, upon occasion, touch a fly from the ears of their horses, shining like satin in the sun."[1]

The Four-in-Hand Club was another free sight of London and although only very rich men could afford to join it most pleasure was probably given to children who could see their "turn outs" on parade in Hyde Park was well as at Epsom on Derby Day. A last goodbye to the old days of coaches, these beautifully kept vehicles, with four matching horses, paraded about London or on the Brighton road. They were to be remembered long after their places had been taken by Rolls Royces, but even in 1900 they were a little quaint, driven by wealthy owners who prided themselves on their spruce appearance and the way in which they held the reins.

Do-gooders were at least trying to make life a little more pleasant for the poorer children.

Missions were usually offshoots of churches in the East End of London. They provided a meeting room where coffee was served, a free library or reading room, many many lectures on rather dull subjects, and they tried to make sure that children had a chance to go to the country.

In 1906 the Fresh Air Fund was formed by Sir Arthur Pearson. Both organisations found places in the country where East End children might have a week or two away from the mean dirty streets. Usually temporary homes would be fixed with country families and so that the town children wouldn't feel out of place they were usually boarded with the families of farm labourers. Poor though they might be, these families had more fresh food than families in town and often their tied cottages gave them more room than the children would be used to in town tenements, where a whole family might live in one room. The cottages were usually cleaner too, for most people who remember living in the poor areas of big cities at this time tell of the ceaseless fight against lice, bugs, fleas and rats.

Some children couldn't even take advantage of offers like these. One girl who went the reverse way — from a mining area during the later Depression to a family in London — described how she thought that she would never be allowed to go away from home because she simply had no clothes at all, or any shoes. Finally, she was rigged out by neighbours in hand-me-downs. Lack of clothes stopped a lot of children from taking advantage of the Mission offers of free holidays with paid fares. And of course, the most neglected children never had a chance, for their parents wouldn't be seen dead at an East End Mission where only the "respectable" poor met.

Besides, any child over ten had a responsible part-time job and couldn't be spared to go gallivanting into the country, even if the offer were free. Now and again a father or mother would try and make a special effort and take their children to the sea for the day. They would save a little bit of extra money by working overtime or by paying into a club which would then arrange a day trip by wagonette. If they came from a part of the city which was better off they might even go to places like Margate, Ramsgate or Broadstairs, travelling by rail excursions or on the river, for boats went up and down the Thames. Glasgow steamers also went down the Clyde on day trips to resorts like Dunoon.

In the North of England days would be spent at Blackpool, Skegness or Scarborough, although "trippers" weren't always very welcome in the last town! Few working families managed more than a day away and sometimes this day would have to keep a child happy for years, as it would be the only time they had a holiday. One small child who went on a day trip to Southend never forgot it. The boy, whose name was Charlie Chaplin, lived with his mother and elder brother Sidney. They were very poor, and most of their food came from charities run by churches and local councils. His mother tried to keep them by taking in needlework but this became too much for her, and although her sons didn't realise it, she would soon break down completely and would be sent to a mental home. The older boy sold newspapers out of school hours, wearing his mother's old velvet jacket and a pair of her high-heeled shoes, cut down to his size. One day he found a purse left on a 'bus seat. Sidney ran home with it. In it were seven gold sovereigns — a fortune to a family like the Chaplins. Their mother rigged them out with new clothes and took them to Southend for the day!

Years later Chaplin wrote: "My first sight of the sea was hypnotic. As I approached it in bright sunlight from a hilly street, it looked suspended, a live quivering monster about to fall on me. The three of us took off our shoes and paddled. The tepid sea unfurling over my insteps and round my ankles and the soft yielding sand under my feet were a revelation of delight.

"What a day that was — the saffron beach, with its pink and blue pails and wooden spades, its coloured tents and umbrellas, and sailing boats hurtling gaily over little waves, and up on the beach other boats resting idly on their sides, smelling of seaweed and tar — a memory of it still lingers with enchantment.

"In 1957 I went back to Southend and looked in vain for the narrow hilly street from which I had seen the sea for the first time, but there were no traces of it. At the end of the town were the remnants of what seemed a familiar fishing village with old-fashioned shop fronts. This had vague whisperings of the past — perhaps it was the odour of seaweed and tar."[2]

1. Shaw Desmond: *The Edwardian Story*. Rockcliff 1949
2. Charles Chaplin: *My Autobiography*. The Bodley Head 1964.

YDE, GLASGOW, FROM SAILORS HOME.

Clyde steamers at Glasgow, 1900.

The country child on holiday. 1900–1914
"Wait for the wagon"

A group of village school girls, 1905.

On holiday you would have seen very quickly how different country life was from town life. Country schools had even longer summer holidays so that the children could help with the harvest. In the early days of this century harvests were not finished in a few days; they could last for weeks depending on the weather and children were very useful, stacking the sheaves of corn into threes and fours where they could wait in little pyramids until the waggons came along and the sheaves were thrown together and carried to the big stacks in the corners of the fields. After harvest there was gleaning and even children who had not helped in the harvest would take part in this because the free grain was welcome when every family had a few hens.

In some villages a bell was rung at eight in the morning to allow the gleaners into the field and rang again at seven at night when they finished. As long as a farmer left one stook of corn in a field the gleaners knew they couldn't enter it. Boys were thought to be a nuisance in the gleaning fields and in one Suffolk village they dressed as girls to get into the field. Anybody who had helped with the harvest was allowed to join the farm family for the Harvest Supper. In many places, especially the north and west, lots of roving workers arrived at harvest time, often from Scotland or Ireland. They slept in barns and most of them looked rough but were in fact skilled at using handrakes and farm machinery. Harvest Supper was nearly always roast beef and plum pudding (rather like Christmas Pudding). Afterwards the long trestle tables would be pushed back or dismantled and the farm people and any villagers who joined them would dance until midnight. Many of the travelling workers were expert clog or jig dancers and some played musical instruments like fiddles or small accordions.

"The farmers wanted cheap labour and the parents wanted money,"[1] and so many village children were hardly ever at school even during term time. There was always some excuse for their absence and teachers turned a blind eye to their truancy because these children had no hope of any work in the future except farm labouring, and they might as well get their hands in while they were young. In "Ask the Fellows who Cut the Hay" George Ewart Evans tells us how children spent these "holidays from school". In January they would be picking stones in the fields, not only to make them easier to cultivate but also because the farmers were paid by the local councils for stones for roadmending. In the next two months they were scaring birds from the crops which were just poking through the earth. Then they would go to school until June when they would be out bird scaring again, swinging great wooden clappers all day on the edge of the field. If the sound of the clapper stopped the farmer's wife would often come out to clip the child's ear. This sounds dreadfully hard to us, but most children seem to have really enjoyed their work in the fields in summer, for they had one or two good farm meals, and before the first world war, when

food was cheap and plentiful in the country, they ate "fit to bust". In July they went "singling", which was hoeing the root crops and thinning them. After that there was sheep shearing when bigger boys were expected to help hold the struggling sheep. In the autumn there were acorn picking days ... very necessary when most families had a pig who would live off acorns. In winter, country children were helping with potato picking and if they were old enough to pick fast they even earned a little money this way. As you see, holidays as we know them were unheard of, and most children enjoyed their days off school even if they meant hard work. They knew that their whole futures would be bound up with the few farms about them.

As motor traffic was hardly ever seen they had no idea that in fact they would be the first generation who could look for work in towns. The only children treated differently were those who would become craftsmen ... blacksmiths, thatchers, butchers. These lucky boys would be allowed to learn a craft which might bring them in more money in the long run, but which meant less wages at the beginning of their working life when they were learning.

Girls were off school even more frequently. Not only for farm work but because there were usually babies at home and when their mothers went out to work in the "big houses" of the village, they would have to mind several children under five. Very little happened in villages during the holidays. A stranger was an event and anybody who passed down the village street was noticed and talked about ... not because villagers were nosey but because they were interested, and so little happened to change their lives. The village shop was the centre for gossip and church and chapel were well attended because they gave the women a chance to meet each other — as well as for religious reasons. Pubs gave the men a chance to get together. Even the children had one or two recognised meeting places where they would all gather on summer days during the holidays and have rather mild adventures. The tree was a usual meeting place ... some

A village outing. Standing room only. 1905.

large oak near the village green with a broken seat around it; or the pond if there was one, where the boys could throw stones across the water and the girls would compare wooden dolls. These meeting places were always near the centre of the village because at any moment a mother might yell "Lizzie-Anne, I want you" . . . and Lizzie would have to run home if she didn't want a smack round the ear hole.

But one great happening in the village was the Sunday School Outing. Sunday Schools in towns had outings as well but they were never remembered like those of the country, probably because it was so rare for a village child to leave home. If there was not much money the outing would be very simple; a farmer would lend a waggon and the children would be driven a few miles to a field belonging to another friendly farmer where they would have a picnic and team games. If the village had a bit more money or if there was a squire who could fork out a few pounds, Sunday School Outings were more ambitious, sometimes with train excursions to the seaside.

As everybody wanted to make the most of their one day holiday the party would usually leave the village early, as early as six o'clock, but as these days were always in July and early August it might already be sunny when the boys and girls would be gathering in the centre of the village. None of them would be dressed suitably for a day by the sea or the country. In fact only a few fairly rich children with advanced parents knew what simple clothes were. The village children would all show their respectability with hats, stockings and starched white clothes. The boys would be wearing scratchy suits with knickerbockers and high stiff collars, and the poor girls — what they suffered! — would have long sausage-shaped ringlets which had been made the night before by tying their hair into curlpapers or rags. Few girls slept the night before the Sunday School Outing, their heads were too sore.

The thought of soft shoes would have shocked their mothers. Sensible families bought boots for boys and girls, the only difference between them being that boys' boots had a toecap, so that they wouldn't suffer from stonekicking. A few "posh" girls might have soft leather boots with laces up to the knees. Richer children wore easier shoes, but then their footwear didn't have to last so long and wouldn't be passed on to younger brothers and sisters.

The girls almost always wore white "for best", and dresses for the Sunday School Outing *were* best. They had layers of clothing, including not only vests, but liberty bodices which were lined with winceyette and had buttons round the bottom onto which their long black stockings were fastened with tapes. Their petticoats were starched until they scratched and if their dresses were not white they might be of serge, a heavy blue wool cloth, and made to look like a sailor dress. "Fashionable" small boys wore sailor suits and hats with the names of ships on the

A holiday fairground.

A country fête.

ribbons but few costumes like these were seen in the villages. Children's clothes were made to last and if they couldn't be washed they were in dark colours, for drycleaning was very rare except among the rich in towns.

A child described her outing from the Forest of Dean. This took place in the 1920s but was not very different from treats before the war: "What travellers we were! It was a good twenty miles ride to our destination, a privately owned playground." It "wasn't a brightly painted affair. But there were see-saws, helter skelters and swings. With our threepence entrance fee we had freedom to go on anything. A tea was laid on in a big wooden hut; not unlimited like the chapel treat tea, but all the same a satisfying number of pieces of bread and butter, a small fancy cake apiece, and two cups of tea. It was stylish too, for we sat on long wooden benches and ate off trestle tables."[2]

Sometimes the country child shared the exotic fairground pleasures which were familiar to town children. If a fair came to the nearest town their families made some effort to take them even if it meant a complicated system of borrowing a horse and trap or sharing a hire of a waggon with other parents. But they would still have a week to think about going to the fair and meanwhile some of the grownups would have slipped off on their own, walking five or six miles to the town and back and thrilling children with stories of all the delights they would see "come Saturday".

"Dan brought news of the fair, of the fine dobby horses and a merry-go-round bigger than ever, with ostriches as well as horses. He went down there at night when he had finished. He swilled his face at the slop-stone (outdoor sink and pump) till it shone in the firelight. He rubbed sweet smelling oil on his hair and parted it carefully at the side before the little rose framed mirror. He put on a clean pink and white rubber collar, and carried a stick in his hand, and a rose in his cap."[3] The fair was set up in the town square with swing boats diving in and out between the houses. Shooting galleries and coconut shies were put up in the streets outside familiar shops. The whole of the central square was taken up with a large and a small roundabout and because it was "wakes" week, the traditional fair of the North of England, spiced biscuits were sold called Wakes Cakes. Country fairs were very cosy for the stall holders travelled a very small circuit and came to know most of the local people.

Diamond Jubilee Year was 1897, when Victoria had been queen for fifty years. It saw a crop of special "do's" which would be remembered forever by most children. To begin with there was the Tea or the Treat. It was to become an annual event. Some villages had special teas before, connected with school or Sunday School, but this year they outshone all the others and children were given mugs with the queen's head on, bags of sweets (a great treat in those days) and in the evening there were firework displays.

"Dolly and Ada were beside themselves with excitement. All the schools had a holiday, and it was a thrill to wear one's best white frock with one's best black stockings and nailed boots."

After tea the squire's daughters sang songs in the open air for the Treat took place in the gardens of the Big House (a very important place in villages at that time). Then there were sports, and Ada, who won the races, was given "Six yards of the unbleached calico which had recently covered the tea tables. It made stout pillow cases for the family which lasted many years and was considered by all to be a practical and most welcome prize." At the end of the day when they all went slowly back home "tired Dolly, clinging to the pram for support, thought she would never forget what a wonderful day. 'Nothing ever happens in Beech Green' she had heard people say. No one could say that now."[4]

This colossal feast paved the way for many other village treats. In the following years there were several big occasions like the coronations of Edward VII and George V, the Armistice, the Silver Jubilee and the coronation of George VI, which would produce treats remembered by many children who took part in them. And with them came lots of mementoes which you may have in your own homes, for every child was given a mug or a milk jug or a beaker which usually had the heads of the king and queen on them. Nowadays they are collected and kept in a place of honour.

But most villages had a special tea once a year even when there was no great national happening. One writer who remembers her village treats says "It was the only time we had enough to eat". It was also often the only time that a village child had shop-bought sweets.

Most country children stored up these events in their minds from one year to another. They never expected to leave their villages and were easily thrilled by visitors, or a long walk to the nearest market town (or, even better, a lift in the trap of a friendly farmer or shopkeeper). Few of our grand-parents resented their stay-at-home holidays and most of them look back on summers in the villages as the happiest times of their lives.

1. George Ewart Evans: *Ask the Fellows who cut the Hay.* Faber 1956
2. Winifred Foley: *A Child of the Forest.* B.B.C. Publications 1974
3. Alison Uttley: *The Country Child.* Faber 1931
4. "Miss Read": *Miss Clare Remembers.* Penguin 1962

A village band, 1914. Source of much entertainment.

Holidays for the well-to-do. 1900–1914
"I do like to be beside the seaside"

"Sunday afternoons ... were always very pleasant, for there were concerts in the Winter Gardens at 3.30. The band, discarding its uniforms, would adopt frock coats, while the conductor would walk round the corner into his glass case, curling a waxed military moustache and sporting a top hat."[1]

All the old ladies would breathe a sigh of pleasure and settle back in their wicker chairs while a smell of violets and discreet colognes floated through the potted palms. This was Scarborough before the first world war, when any people of any pretensions came to the seaside and almost ignored the sea.

But all seaside towns weren't as grand as Scarborough. Early in the century they had to decide what they *were* going to be like because although there were many people who couldn't visit the sea there were lots of others who did. A skilled workman managed the odd day off when he could go on a day excursion. Shopkeepers might put up their shutters for a week or leave an assistant in charge while they had a holiday; and in many parts of the country there were weeks when the whole town would close down for "Wakes" week and even if the men who did poorly paid jobs couldn't get away, those who earned a little more could manage either a day or a week at the sea. Lots of the people who took advantage of cheap holiday fares on the train were young and unmarried and were living the best years of their lives.

The big question in seaside towns was: "Are we going to be 'select' or not?" If they were "select" it meant they had chosen to be a quiet town, visited by those who wanted to stay in a place with no noisy entertainments. But it also meant that less money came into the town because day trippers wouldn't visit it. Some seaside resorts realised that if they became more "common" they would make more money. It was lucky that they did because children generally enjoyed these brightly lit towns more than the "select" ones. Once the idea of cheap day excursions by trains had caught on, the brasher seaside towns began to boom. Blackpool was the most adventurous. It had three piers and a big Ferris wheel of the type which had become popular as the "flip-flap" in Paris in 1870. And there was another thing Blackpool had copied from Paris, its very own Eiffel Tower. Very soon the town was bursting with tourists, most of whom came for the day by train. Blackpool's visitors came from the Lancashire cotton mill towns but London also had its very important seaside town, Southend. Even when Charlie Chaplin had visited it at the turn of the century it had been partly a fishing village and had smelt of tar and brine. In 1898 Southend Council built the largest pier in the world which stretched out into the sea like an outsize finger, over a mile of it, and if you were too old or too young to walk that far, there was a tram to the very end. Edwardians loved piers which took them out over the sea so that they could smell the salt air and see the water lapping under them while they didn't wet their feet. Most of

24

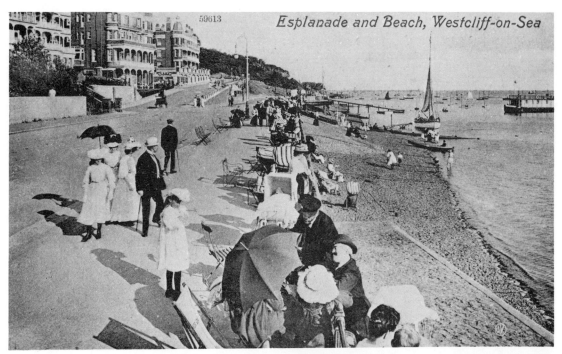

59613

Esplanade and Beach, Westcliff-on-Sea

The 'posh' seaside, Westcliff-on-Sea.

these piers are still standing and some are very attractive with curly wrought iron work on the lamp posts and pretty spikey buildings in which there are amusement arcades or theatres. Very often, in resorts which were more popular than Scarborough, the band didn't stay in the Winter Gardens — which were huge glass conservatories — but went to the end of the pier where they played in wooden bandstands. The musicians were often dressed up in very elaborate uniforms. And as they belted out the latest hit tunes, carriages passed up and down the promenades, which were the long roads fronting the sea. Horses and cabs were to last longer at the seaside than anywhere else, because their leisurely pace went so well with sunshine and sea air. The children could have rides in goat carts or on donkeys.

Behind the continual passing of elegant ladies and polite gentlemen you might have seen builders at work on new hotels. Hotels had not been thought very respectable until 1900. Travellers had rarely stayed longer than a night. Most seaside visitors "took rooms" which meant several bedrooms for

H.M. KING EDWARD VII.   Copyright.

King Edward VII.

25

Donkey rides on Blackpool beach, 1906.

the children and parents, and a sitting room. They brought their own servants. Even quite poor families would have a maid to look after the children. But now that more and more people packed into the seaside towns, boarding houses began to offer less accommodation and to make more money. New hotels were built like the Metropole at Brighton, where five millionaires could be seen chatting in the foyer at a time, and where the three best suites stretched over the first three floors. Here would come Mama, Papa, the governess, the lady's maid, the valet, the nurse and the children. Sailing was the great pleasure of the rich Edwardians because the Royal Family not only spent a good part of the summer at Cowes in the Isle of Wight, but also encouraged their royal cousins to visit them there, so that the Russian Czar and the German Kaiser arrived with their households. Important people of this sort brought their own luxurious steam yachts and stayed at sea but their presence en-

couraged hangers-on who went to the large hotels in the areas.

This was a time when the rich were not thought vulgar as they had been in the time of Queen Victoria. Edward VII enjoyed extravagant pleasure-seeking people around him and as he moved from one part of the country to another his friends — who formed what was called Society in those days — went with him. And many people who hoped to be his friends went along too. So hotels sprang up wherever he went; in the Highlands of Scotland where he went for shooting, and rich people built hunting lodges in which they would spend a few weeks of the year; in the South of France where hotels and villas were built in what had been very quiet fishing villages; and in the big German spas. Forty years before only the poor but genteel English had gone to these places; those who wanted to keep up appearances and couldn't afford to live well in England had fled to France and Germany where living had been very cheap.

Edward VII made it fashionable to go abroad for holidays.

Like flocks of migrating birds the members of Society flew behind their king, and wherever he touched down, they did too, and opulent hotels were built.

Older people still thought that hotels were rather daring. They knew that food was badly cooked and that *anybody* might speak to you on the stairs, so they rented or built houses in towns like Nice and Cannes. So many British spent winter in the South of France that the big main road on the sea front at Nice was called the English Promenade (Promenade des Anglais).

The wealthy travelled with their servants and lots of bags and baggage, but there were other people who wanted to go abroad with less fuss and expense. Sixty years before, a young man called Thomas Cook had been rather annoyed at having to walk fifteen miles to a meeting he wanted to attend in Leicester. He had decided that next time he would ask lots of his friends if they wanted to visit similar meetings and if enough agreed he would hire a train for them. It had been the first "package deal" trip, and by 1900 Thomas Cook was well known in the travel business. This company could fix visits anywhere in the world providing enough

Clovelly; the quiet seaside.

people wanted to go together. They took the first English to Switzerland, they had even had the cheek to hire a boat which went up the Nile close behind that of the Prince of Wales in 1869. Most of their customers were quite well-off because going abroad *was* expensive even with cut price rates: vicars, doctors, and teachers made up most of their groups.

At the turn of the century some holiday trips were arranged by the Regent Street Polytechnic. This was the first "tech" and had been opened so that young men who wanted to "better" themselves could have lessons and lectures in the evenings after they had finished work. By 1898, 6,000 people a year went abroad through "Poly Tours". They made no profit which might explain their cheapness. For nine guineas they would take you to Norway for thirteen days. If you were less well-off there was a five guinea trip to Switzerland which lasted eight days. "Poly Tours" was popular enough for them to build their own chalets at Lucerne in Switzerland.

These were all holidays for grownups. Where did the children of the rich go in the summer?

Most families rented a house by the sea. In those days many parents saw very little of their children and often the children were closer to their nanny or governess than to their mother. While the very rich parents were jaunting round Europe behind the king, the children would stay in some quiet place like Weymouth or the little known villages on the Devon and Cornish coast. Their days would be spent digging in the sand or hunting for shells and shellfish. Like the poorer children they didn't expect to be amused during their holidays, it was enough to be in a strange place. It took some time for a family to settle when they rented a house. If they were middle class children their mothers would be with them, with perhaps one nursemaid to help her. Linen was brought from their own houses in big wooden boxes. The holiday houses were often very badly furnished and not very modern even for those

Bathing huts at Bexhill-on-Sea, 1913.

dress and hang their clothes up. A ramp led from the sea end of the hut into the water so that nervous holiday makers needn't get more than their feet wet by dangling them over the side. If you were very prudish you could have a sort of enclosed canopy fitted to your machine like a tent which covered you when you went into the water. But not much of you would be seen anyway.

Most seaside towns had their own rules about bathing. There were men's beaches and the opposite sex wasn't allowed within twenty or thirty yards from the other's beach. Ladies *had* to be covered from the neck to the knees and even had to have a skirt over their costume. This was often a frill which echoed the bathing hat, which was also frilled like today's shower cap. The bathing costume had sleeves and leggings down to the knee and in 1900 it was always made of the same prickly serge which was used for children's sailor suits. Most children hated their bathing costumes and avoided the sea because they could not bear wearing these hot clinging horrors which became heavy

days. They would have no gas lighting but candles or oil lamps which would be tiresome to families who were used to living in towns. Cooking would be on an open range, and as quietness was supposed to be one of the pleasures of a holiday they were often some way from the nearest village. There was such turmoil in moving to a holiday house that most families stayed at least a month to make it worthwhile.

If the children stayed in a seaside town they had to be very careful how they dressed. They could never appear off the beach in a swim suit or bathing dress, as it was called then. They dressed and undressed in beach huts or tents. These had been in use since the early years of the century and many seaside households also had their own bathing machine on wheels which was pulled into the water by a donkey, or an enormous bathing machine woman who also ducked the children in the water to get them used to the sea. Not surprisingly most children were terrified of the bathing machine woman who became a bogey to them. The machines were quite big inside to that two people could un-

Westcliff-on-Sea Promenade.

and smelt of damp wool when wet. Boys had to cover their bodies up in the same way although they were spared the skirts.

After bathing, you did not sit in the sun. Pink and white skins were very proper and a bronzed skin suggested gipsies or, perhaps worse, foreigners, so sunbathing was not allowed and if children wanted to potter about on the beach they wore hats to protect their faces, and their mothers or nurses had sunshades. Ladies occasionally paddled but couldn't go in very far as they were expected not to show more than an ankle and above this they would be in a thick serge or flannel skirt and a "shirtwaister", which was a blouse which was almost always worn at the seaside. Gentlemen wore three piece suits, although a few daring men managed to get away with flannel trousers and blazers, with a boater or straw hat, of course. Only very common people went out with bared heads.

Pierrots were to become very popular at the seaside but before 1914 there were not many shows on the beach except the Punch and Judy man. This show, or variations of it, had been acted out for many years and although the story was always the same with the characters of Punch, Judy, the dog Toby, the policeman and the hangman, children would watch it over and over again, not at all worried by its blood-thirsty story. Each seaside town of any size had its own Punch and Judy man with a booth which was permanently on the beach. Boats were wedged between bathing machines and tents. These were still very obvious at the seaside because fishermen were still working off those beaches from which children paddled, and heavy tarred boats, smelling of fish and encrusted with barnacles, would be pulled up on the shingle during the afternoons. Any entertainment for visitors was very amateur and left to the local landladies and fishermen, so that an exciting day out was often a picnic or a trip out to sea to catch your own high tea. Seaside landladies had a reputation for being tight-fisted and cantankerous. Most of them had large houses from which they earned a

The Grand Pier at Weston-super-Mare, 1912.

A typical seaside boarding house in this case at Margate. Such a group snapshot would be treasured for many years by the guests.

precarious living with the meagre help of one servant. In a novel called *The Climber* an Edwardian writer called E. F. Benson describes the typical seaside house of 1908:

"Sea View was a house in a row of sounding titles. On one side of them was Blenheim, and the other Balmoral while farther down was Engadine, Chatsworth and the houses of Devonshire and Stafford. Six rather steep steps led from a small clanging gate to the front door, which had panels of stained glass in it. On one side was the drawing room, which Elizabeth had made quite homey with a quantity of woollen headrests, here really necessary, since without them the person who reclined on the American-cloth sofa would have instantly slid off onto the floor. ... In the bow window, rather obstructing the view out, but equally obstructing the view of those without who wished to look in, was a marine telescope on three brass legs, which Aunt Elizabeth vaguely felt should have its cap permanently put on to it because of the bathers.

It was true you need not look at the bathers, but if you did they would appear so unpleasantly near. ... A barometer and an umbrella-stand naturally stood in the hall, the former of a pessimistic nature that silently clung to the fact that it was 'stormy'. But the whole house was, except when the kitchen door had been left open, redolent of the freshness of the sea, and Lucia, who had again secured a bedroom at the very top of the house, lived as in the deck-cabin of a ship."

Visitors accepted a certain amount of discomfort as the price they had to pay for a seaside holiday. In fact they even seem to have enjoyed the sand-strewn halls, the uncomfortable dining rooms in which nobody ever spoke, the dull food and sometimes, the lack of hygiene. It was part of the fun of a holiday. In *The Diary of a Nobody* the Pooters go to their "digs" by the sea, taking with them their fashionable young son, Lupin, who is very critical of his parents' habits. This was written at the end of the nineteenth century but seaside behaviour did not change:

"August 13th. Hurrah! at Broadstairs. Very nice apartments near the station. On the cliffs they would have been double the price. The landlady had a nice five o'clock dinner and tea ready which we all enjoyed, though Lupin seemed fastidious because there happened to be a fly in the butter. . . .

"August 16th. Lupin positively refused to walk down the parade with me because I was wearing my new straw helmet with my frock coat. I don't know what the boy is coming to.

"August 17. Lupin not falling in with our views, Carrie and I went for a sail. It was a relief to be with her alone, for when Lupin irritates me she always sides with him. On our return, he said: 'Oh you've been on the Shilling Emetic have you? You'll come to a six-pennorth on the Liver Jerker next.' I presume he meant a tricycle, but I affected not to understand him."

Cycling was the great leisure sport of the time. In the 1890s girls and young men had seen bicycles as a way to get away from home unchaperoned, even for a short time, and many true and fictitious love stories grew up round cycles with flat tyres, cyclists who lost their way or unwary cyclists who fell in the ditch! Daring and fast, the daughters of the family fled from their homes on summer afternoons, to cycle furiously about the countryside. They even wore "rational dress" to cycle! This was rather shocking as it was breeches or bloomers of heavy serge, worn with a blouse and a straw boater hat. Seaside towns always had a hiring cycle shop from which apprehensive novice cyclists would wheel out iron framed "boneshakers". It's almost impossible for us to imagine how the bicycle became a symbol of freedom. It was at first too expensive for poor people, only those who were fairly well off could afford it. And it was not used in a very practical way, for few people rode cycles to work and there was no need to use them for shopping, as everything was delivered. No, they were for leisure. Cycling tracks were made in the big parks and the country lanes became more dangerous than ever before as new owners

of bicycles wobbled their way along, in an age when keeping to one side of the road hardly mattered. Motor cars were not used for holiday travel unless you were very rich and cars were thought rather comical, for most of them were seen at the side of the road, with bonnets up, waiting for an important and usually unavailable spare part. In those days, cars came with chauffeurs, for only a driver trained by the car manufacturer could be expected to pamper his expensive, uncomfortable, noisy and smelly object which travelled at about 15 miles an hour, passed occasionally by cyclists and horses. No wonder most people thought the car was not here to stay! Of course, bicycles could be ridden in town and at weekends, not only on holidays, but adventurous young men were already going on cycling and camping tours, with a few possessions crammed into their saddle bags. They seemed to have unlimited energy and to enjoy the struggle of walking up steep hills in order to cruise down on the other side in the days when there were no gear shifts.

Discomfort might have accompanied cam-

The Bandstand, Westcliff-on-Sea.

ping but if you had enough money it need not. In the early years of the century it was considered part of a summer's evening fun to camp along by the Thames near Henley, especially when the boat races were on. "Men only" might have been written up over the tents for few girls wanted to suffer mosquitoes and the chancy water supply of camping. And yet, these tents were grander than any until our own time, with lighting, carpets on board floors, and proper dining tables. The British camper learned a lot from the outposts of the Empire, and luxurious tents were among the lesson. Some businessmen even commuted from their tents into London by rail.

Holidays at home.

You might say that it was difficult to see where everyday life ended and holidays began for the richer people. It's true that papas went to the office, unless they had unearned incomes, but few if any middle class mamas worked and as their housework was done by other people you might think they would have lots of time to spend with their children. In fact they hardly saw them unless they were very unusual, and to admit that they took care of their own children would have made most Edwardian mothers outcasts because there were careful rules about the upbringing of the family. When a baby was born it had a nanny. As more children were added, the older nanny became the "boss" nurse and had a nursery maid working under her who made up the fires and carried the children's meals from the kitchen in the basement to the nursery at the top of the house. She also carried the children's bath water in big enamel or brass cans. The children would

On the sands at Eastbourne, 1915.

An Oxford Hip Bath.

bathe in hip baths before the nursery fire which was often lit even in the summer, with a brass railed fireguard before it on which clothes could air. When the children became older they had a nursery governess, who taught them lessons until the boys went to school. Many girls never left home but were taught by another governess when they were over seven. Often the older nanny never left the family, but stayed until the children were grown up, then took care of *their* children.

Most nannies are remembered as domineering, old and vicious, for with complete control over the children and the undermaid, they could become tyrannical. In more humble homes there was often only one available maid who found time, when she was not cleaning or laying tables, to accompany the children when they went for "treats". Very often this girl was not much older than the children she cared for, and they became very friendly. Accompanied by their "Edith", "Alice", or "Annie" the children could enjoy all the delights of winters in town too. And there were lots of holiday trips for richer children.

The zoo was one of the most popular places, as it is now, and had very much the same amusements, with elephant and camel rides. Madame Tussaud's was another place to go on a wet day but because it became rather crowded many mothers refused permission for their children to visit the waxworks in case they picked up an illness.

This was a more possible danger than we would imagine today, because typhoid, diphtheria and scarlet fever were still common ailments from which many children died each year. So perhaps the mamas were not being foolish and priggish. The children of richer families never went to common places like fairs but then London was full of the oddest theatre shows which people flocked to, although we might find some of them rather sinister today. There were midgets and giants, hypnotists and acrobats but the most popular shows of all were given by Maskelyne and Devant, two "magicians" who played to packed houses. Many boys had conjuring sets for Christmas after they had visited their famous shows at the Egyptian Hall. A new trick was an event, and would be written up in newspapers like a play is today.

The *Strand Magazine* gave away the secret of Devant's trick of the "Spirit Wife", excusing the fact that they had let the cat out of the bag by saying that they were sure an explanation would make Mr. Devant's show an even greater success:

"Mr Devant simulates grief, and suddenly feels the power to bring before him the spirit of his absent wife. And so the vision floats before him, graceful, transparent, mysterious. And this is how it is done:—

"'The principle' says Mr Devant 'is simple reflection. The stage is entirely covered with a huge sheet of very clear plate glass, and as the audience see everything through this, they don't suspect its presence. Miss Maria Melville, who enacts the part of the spirit, is placed on a black velvet couch beneath the stage and a little in front of it — in fact where the orchestra usually sit. The couch can be readily moved into any position by mechanical means. A powerful electric light is cast upon the reclining figure of the lady, and the lights behind the plate glass are slightly lowered'. A ghostly reflection is at once visible, and of course, Mr Devant is seen through it."

America had the most outrageous sideshows, which seem to have been filled with fat ladies, dogfaced men, human skeletons and underwater snake charmers, most of them employed by the famous showman, Barnum. But British theatres had their own attractions. Like Zazel, a lady who was paid £100 a week to be shot from a cannon at the Royal Aquarium; or John Chambers, the Armless Wonder who used his feet in place of hands during his performance; or there was the greatest juggler in the world, Paul Cinquevalli . . . After performing before the Prince of Wales (later Edward VII) at Marlborough House, he was considered "suitable" entertainment for children. He could stop a 48lb. cannon ball, which was hurtling towards him, with the side of a plate. One of Cinquevalli's tricks was inspired by a very English picnic on the river. "One summer I was up the Thames picnicking with a party of friends. At Marlow we left the launch, and on the bank there we spread the cloth. Later I commenced juggling as usual with everything within reach — sardine

boxes, glasses, serviettes and so on. Then I picked up an umbrella and presently a bottle half full of lemonade. After juggling these in various ways, I threw up the bottle, opened the umbrella while it was descending and received it (the top) upon the ferrule, while it poured out its contents . . ." Cinquevalli says nothing of his friends' reaction; were they applauding? Or cursing because they had lost their lemonade?

Often these entertainers could be seen in purely children's shows, the pantomime. The principal boys of the Edwardian age were, quite unlike any since. They were very dashing of course, for no woman normally showed her legs and they were covered from waist to toes in pink tights. Up above they were less well covered because photographs show them with enormous expanses of naked bosom. They look very fat to us today, but ladies at that time had "hour glass figures" which meant they were shaped like the figure 8. They were much older than principal boys

A group of Black and White Minstrels from Margate. (Radio Times Hulton Picture Library.)

in today's pantomimes because no young girl would have sauntered onto the stage covered with pink silk and spangles.

Pantomimes had only recently stopped being the traditional Harlequin and Colombine shows with serious music and ballets, and had begun to have comedians who produced strings of sausages out of their hats and threw buckets of white-wash at each other.

"The Black and White Minstrels" were another show thought suitable for children. All the performers were, of course, white men wearing extravagant painted faces and the traditional striped trousers and toppers which we see the minstrels in today. Originally the most famous troupe had been the Christy Minstrels in the days of Queen Victoria, but in the years when Edwardian children visited these shows they were the Moore and Burgess Minstrels who played in the St James' Hall in Piccadilly and who were so popular that those unfortunates, who had too little money to have expensive seats booked for them, would sit on the pavements with mattresses and bedclothes until they could get into the gallery or the pit of the theatre.

Children simply did not see the most moving theatrical shows which were the music halls. Poor children could not afford them and the rich would not have been allowed by their parents to see those rather shocking rollicking noisy performances by great comedians and singers of the time.

Older children might go out to a theatre in the evening to see musical shows in the years before 1914, when the D'Oyley Carte Company would be playing the Gilbert and Sullivan Operas at the Savoy Theatre. These have been "on stage" ever since they were first written and if you have a chance to go and see them, you will be hearing jokes and listening to songs which amused children and grownups in the 1870s.

Going to the theatre was quite a performance in itself. If the family didn't have its own carriage, a cab would be hired for the evening from a livery stable. Very often the

'Bubbles' by Sir John Millais. One of the most famous advertisements in this period.

cabman would have taken the family out so often that they would know him and he might even be a regular caller on the cook in the kitchen. Hansoms, growlers or four wheelers might be used depending on the size of the family and the one thing common to them all was that they jingled all the time when the harness moved. The floors inside would be covered with straw, to keep the passengers' feet warm, and a rug would be supplied too, to cover their knees. Sometimes an "apron" front closed over them. Cabs always smelt of horse liniment, old polished leather and even dung . . . and nearly everybody who rode in them felt sad when they went, and the more noisy, less cosy taxis took their places.

When you reached the theatre there would be no ices offered. After all, refrigeration had only recently come into general use. Large families might sit in a box, although then they would only see one side of the stage

35

clearly. Most theatres were very much as they are today for many of them have deliberately kept their Edwardian good looks, with lots of gilt paint, carved figures, and red or deep blue plush seats. In those days everybody who sat below the upper circle wore evening dress. An older daughter of the family might even be allowed to "put her hair up" for a visit to a theatre. At sixteen girls were expected to lift their long hair into buns on top of their heads and this showed they were growing up.

If they were not in a box the children might be unlucky for not only did adult ladies put their hair up, but they also filled them with feathers and flowers when they visited the theatre so that a small child behind them would hardly see anything. Ladies' dresses were very low cut. The men wore tailcoats and starched white collars with white bow ties. In those days anybody who was rich enough to have servants . . . and that was a great number of people . . . would also probably have enough money to go out in the evenings, and to wear evening clothes.

If the children were very spoilt they might be allowed to stay up late and visit an ice cream parlour. These were Italian, and the most famous were Gatti's and Frascati's. The ices were made of pure fruit juice, eggs and cream, and for most children they remained one of the most exciting memories of going out in the evening. However, they would not eat out. Dining in restaurants was a man's pleasure. Ladies never ate out in the evening and certainly children did not. A few department stores were beginning to serve teas and lunches which were meant for their female customers. The women kept to their tea rooms and the men to their restaurants. It was like going to separate beaches to bathe.

1. "Low Tide" from The Collected Stories: Osbert Sitwell. Macmillan 1953.

The South Pier at Lowestoft.

After the war was over. 1918–1919
"When the lights go on again . . . ."

We think of the First World War as a terrible disaster in which many men died in the muddy trenches of Northern France; but we forget that at home lots of people were living very much as they had before the war. Even if their husbands and fathers were far away there was none of the panic which made families scatter to the country as they would in the Second World War.

Although women went to work in munitions factories and on the land they were usually single women or had no children. Mothers who had always worked in factories still went to them and made more money than they ever had before. Fashions changed because bobbed hair didn't get caught up in machinery, and shorter skirts were more sensible for the girls who did war work. Women working on the land were even able to wear riding breeches and get away with it. It was all in the cause of helping the war effort.

Middle class mothers rolled bandages and did a little hospital visiting. A lot of this was done at the seaside, for big houses overlooking the sea became convalescent homes for wounded soldiers, and so did a lot of mansions in the country. Quite a few of them would never be private homes again.

Those who had always had holidays still expected to go away in July and August even if the men of the family were fighting abroad. However, very few went to the East Coast. For many years before the war seaside resorts like Frinton, Bridlington and Cromer had been very popular but they lost their visitors during the war when the Germans possessed parts of the Belgian coast and began to shell English seaside towns. They did remarkably little harm at such long range, but they did make life disturbing. Poor elegant Scarborough with its largely elderly wartime population suffered most of all:

"The noise of the great naval guns thumping and crashing through the mist, which magnified the sound, was enormous. It was about 8.15 a.m., my father was just dressing, and lost no time in finishing the process and getting downstairs. A piece of shell went through the front door, piercing a wooden pillar, and buried itself in the smaller hall, while many fragments penetrated into the house. The Swiss footman went upstairs and watched the attack from the roof. My mother, who was in bed when the bombardment took place, refused to move. . . ."[1]

And yet the South Coast towns, well away from the fury of the German guns and with no suspicious offshore boats (which were often proved to be no more than fishing vessels from Lowestoft or Yarmouth), collected all those visitors who could get away from the towns.

Various newspapers adopted the technique of stopping people in the street and asking their views on taking holidays in wartime, and surprisingly many of them thought it was a good idea, their main reaction being "Why should we let a war put us out?" In

Scarborough before the Bombardment.

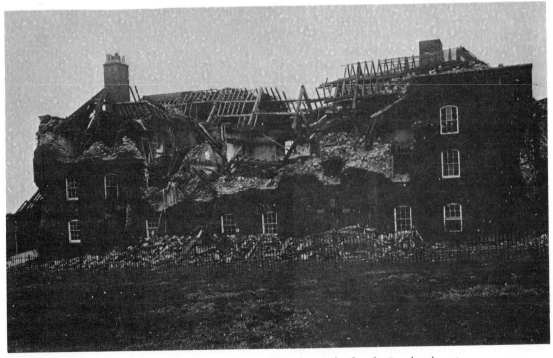

The Barracks, Castle Yard, Scarborough after the Bombardment.

38

August 1915, *The Times* said that Brighton was as crowded as ever but very quiet, except for the children.

The *Daily Mirror* fashion writer even managed to make these notes in 1916: "Bathing gowns are no longer the unsophisticated garments of yore (the past). What stockinette failed to effect, a thick crepe de chine will accomplish. It does not spoil in the water, and a longish sports coat to match thrown over after the bathe, makes as complete a shore suit as one can desire."

Crêpe de chine is a clinging silky material, so you can see that ideas about covering up your body were changing fast, but not too fast — for some years after the war ladies still had to cover their swimsuits with a cape or the "sportscoat" when they came out of the water. They couldn't lie about on the beach in a swimsuit.

In 1918 came the Armistice, and it was very soon obvious that ideas about holidays had changed. Many of the men who had marched away to fight in 1914 had never been further than their own villages, and had been quite content with their backward lives, ruled by the squire, the vicar and rich farmers. And men from towns had been used to having very little work and living from hand to mouth. But when they came back in 1918 they wanted better wages, better houses, proper food and — among the other goodies enjoyed by their "betters" in the past — holidays.

Driving cars in the war had made many of them anxious to have their own motor and from being a rich man's hobby, the car became the family "baby" . . . a small car which went a long way on a gallon of petrol and cost very little to buy.

These were to be made in the 1920s. The immediate needs for holidays after the war had to be catered for in the more accepted way . . . by travelling on trains.

In August 1919 many families prepared for what was to be their first holiday. With father recently returned from the army they might be a tight little group on any railway platform. A small group, for families were to be smaller after 1918, with perhaps only two children. They would look very different from a town family of four or five years before. To begin with, they would be more alert, they would read copies of "cheap" newspapers; years of fighting might have made the man look older than he really was, and he would look determined. He has a steady job bringing in perhaps £2.50 a week. His suit (for he would never wear casual clothes for an outing by the sea) cost about £1.50. He looks determined and he is, absolutely determined that his son and daughter will never run about the town barefoot and turn cartwheels for farthings in the city streets as *he* did when a boy. He wants his children to go to school and "better" themselves. He wants to move out of the grimy two roomed flat he rents at a few shillings a week. His wife, dressed in spotted cotton with strapped white buckskin shoes and a floppy straw hat, also has her dream. She *knows* where they will move to, a semi-detached house on a main road out of town, nearer the fields, and very respectable, where the neighbours will keep their front gardens neat and make tea with each other and the children will grow up to speak properly. A house like that will cost £5 downpayment and then 60p a week on mortgage but she is determined to have it, even if she has to go back to work as a shop assistant.

The children, hopping from one foot to another as they wait for the train, have things few pre-war children of their type would have known about . . . buckets and spades, a doll for the little girl, a cheap cricket hat for the boy. Toys are now thought to be a priority for children.

When the train comes in there is such a crowd! Nobody has ever seen anything like it before . . . but then neither of the parents have ever seen an August Bank Holiday crowd before. They stare at each other, but four years in the trenches have taught Mr how to take care of himself. He opens a carriage door and throws in two cases, then he pushes his wife and children in. The compartment is packed. It may be a G.W.R. train which means most people will stay on it until they reach the coast. All regions have their own railway company, and the Great Western travels west from Paddington. The L.M.S. is the London, Midland and Scottish, and there is the L.N.E.R., the London and North Eastern. They all have distinctively coloured carriages, green, or dark blue or deep red, with their company signs painted on in gilt lettering. Inside, the carriages are rather stuffy. The seats are padded with horsehair and plushily uncomfortable. If you hit one, dust will rise. Above each seat is a photograph of the beauties to be seen from that region's line. The Great Western will probably show the sands at Paignton and Winchester Cathedral. The pictures are pale brown. Between each couple of photographs is a looking glass with G.W.R. on it. The carriage is so full that Mrs is lucky to squeeze into the only vacant seat and to take her daughter on her knee. The other passengers look at her disapprovingly. Passengers always do when newcomers make them push closer on the seat. Mr pushes their cases into the corridor, for the luggage racks are full, and he and his son sit on them for most of the journey. In between mopping their faces and trying to open the closed and jammed windows, the passengers say "Have you ever known it to be so crowded?" — that is if they speak at all.

Mr, Mrs and their two children do not know that they are travelling on the worst holiday they will ever know. In fact it is amazing that the experiences of August 1919 didn't put the British off holidays by the sea for ever.

Most of the visitors had no notion of how one took a holiday. The actual mechanics of it were so new to them. They didn't book rooms, they didn't go to towns that they knew. They don't seem to have considered that the first Bank Holiday after a war would

Waiting for the trippers at Filey, 1919.

Bathers and paddlers at Weymouth in 1919.

be like a small war itself. Mr, Mrs and their children may have been wise to go west. Most Londoners went to resorts near home with appalling results. Fifty thousand went to Yarmouth. All the rooms were taken in Clacton and still thirty five thousand people wandered the streets with nowhere to go. The biggest resort had the worst crowds, for three hundred thousand decided to go to Blackpool. The lucky ones were those who saw what was happening and took the first train out of the town again.

But in those East Coast towns which had been silent and empty for the war years, holiday visitors walked the windy streets all night, or slept in shelters on the front where their summer clothes offered little comfort against the cold sea winds. Many landladies invited extra guests to sleep in the bath or on sofas. And in some towns the police stations were opened so that women and children might sleep in the cells.

When day came there was no let up for the frustrated holiday makers. Many of them could not wash or shave and queued for breakfasts in cafes on the front. The beaches were covered with visitors, their numbers swollen by those who came for the day and found the town occupied by overnight guests who wished they had stayed at home. Those who had hardly seen the sea before, and who had come to Clacton or Margate as the big treat of the year, tried to catch up on the sleep they had lost during the night, by lying on the crowded beaches wherever they could find a space. Queues stood by the water's edge waiting for a chance to paddle or swim.

And yet that terrible Bank Holiday did not put them off, it established that many many more people would visit the seaside than ever before and that now people of all incomes would try to get down to the sea on their days off.

The owners of boarding houses and hotels quickly realised how times were changing and a whole industry began to grow up round the holiday maker. Places which had only interested a few became "Tourist Spots"

41

and little snack bars, car parks and ice cream stalls sprang up like mushrooms in some of the places which had never attracted more than a few scholars before or those amateur artists who painted the Cheddar Gorge or Ann Hathaway's cottage.

Another type of holiday was begun in that summer of 1919, a much more gloomy one. Trips were organised for those who had lost relatives in the war, and they were taken out in parties to visit the trenches. What made their visits really macabre was that in many places the litter of war had not been cleared away, although the bodies of the dead had been filed away in neat cemeteries all over Northern France. The families of the dead soldiers would picnic in those trenches where their sons or husbands had heard the sound of gunfire and from which they had seen flares light up the sky. They sat on the packing cases which had been used as benches by departed soldiers and ate their sandwiches off the field desks supplied by the army. It was all very sad but as long as there were survivors from the war these coach trips would be made every summer. They were usually arranged by Old Comrades Associations, or the British Legion.

The people who had gone to the South of France for holidays before the war, returned, relieved to find that Nice and Cannes were very little changed and still had a charming Edwardian atmosphere. Some of the rich went for later holidays, and a new pleasure called "Winter Sports". The most fashionable resort was St. Moritz where visitors skated, for skiing was still only a necessary method for mountaineers and shepherds to travel from one place to another.

Country house parties started again for they had been stopped because of the shortage of food during the war . . . and the shortage of young men. Now they had a sort of wild gaiety which was very unlike the placid Huntin', Shootin' and Fishin' parties of the past. Some of the people who met in country houses had dances after breakfast and actually pranced about to jazz music. What was the world coming to?

At the skating rink. It's all a question of balance!

"The Country House Party" was to become a godsend to writers of the 1920s, and many plays and detective stories were to be written about these odd high jinks. After all, in what other place could a novelist have eight or nine people, all of "amusing" characters, as well as the servants, who could all be under suspicion for a crime? And to make the plot even more chilling these unpleasant holidays always seemed to occur during floods, heavy snows or some other natural breakdown of communications so that the people in the country house were cut off from the outside world. Any normal reader who was foolish enough to believe in these stories might suppose that certain people in Britain did nothing more than move from one house to another, having perpetual holidays and being waited on by a butler, footman and a whole group of below stairs servants. In fact this pleasant view of a world in which only the servants did any work had been knocked badly by the war and the "country house party" would soon disappear, even as an occasional holiday.

At first the most amazing difference in holidays at home might have been the Americianisms which crept into the British seaside resorts and fairgrounds, such as neon lights, amusement arcades and gramophones playing jazz music.

Before the war the teashop had been a place where the lady typist had her cup of tea and sandwich during lunchtime, but after the war many more people who were not very rich began to eat out. Seaside towns soon had a rash of cafes along the fronts facing the sea, and main roads had transport cafes where the drivers of lorries could have a rest and a meal. And as more and more families bought cars there were more and more day trippers who used these little cafes for their main meals of the day, or who picnicked in beauty spots. Until the cheap cars were made most of these beauty spots had been very quiet and were only visited by local people or those who could manage train fares from towns but as private cars were used, many popular places like Box Hill in Surrey would come alive like an ant heap on Sundays and holidays. There were two ways of looking at this: did you want many people to have a chance to enjoy fresh air and to see woods and streams? Or did you want to keep the countryside fresh and green with no litter in it? The arguments are still going on today.

To begin with most of the visitors were well-to-do. They were the only people who could afford cars and they were very aware of the ugly sight of empty paper bags and bottles because they were used to owning large gardens and fields where they would have resented rubbish. But as 'bus loads came to beauty spots the picture changed, not because the trippers were more dirty but because they weren't used to tramping about in fields and woods and didn't know about

A village outing in 1918 meant a treat for all.

210 ANTIBES
La Rue Saint-Esprit

H. Berger et Cie, Antibes

Antibes, France; popular for holidays.

closing gates and not dropping litter. The changes made lots of country people very angry, especially as so many visitors from town were young couples. Of course older people have always grumbled about "the young ones" and said they are flippant and noisy but immediately after the first world war they really felt they had something to complain about. Not only did the young ones arrive in the country atrociously dressed (or so their elders thought), but also often riding motorbikes. They wore the latest "gear" and you might be surprised to find that this was the jumper, or sweater.

Many girls had grown bored with knitting socks for soldiers and decided to try something for themselves, and so they knitted long tubular pullovers. They even went so far as to knit copies for their men friends so that the first unisex garment appeared in 1919 and shocked and enraged their parents. It was so . . so . . so *casual*, they said. And that was just the clue for everything that young people did or said after the war. They could be easy going, and careless. Many of them were earning more money than their parents had ever dreamed of, and they were doing new jobs too . . . typing, working as mechanics, travelling to serve in smart shops instead of the corner grocers where their mothers might have found work . . . the young men had greased their hair and puffed at gaspers or cheap cigarettes, which they had learned to smoke in the trenches. The girls, who wore makeup and short skirts — or at least shorter than had ever been seen before — were called flappers. They rode on "flapper brackets" on the backs of their boyfriends' noisy motorbikes. They danced daring dances like the Charleston at "roadhouses". These were brightly lit, very expensive pubs with dance bands which were opened on the main roads out of big cities, to take advantage of the new trade of passing motorists.

For a year or two after the war, holidays abroad appealed to only the very rich who had been accustomed to going overseas before. Switzerland was deserted in 1920. On August 25th a writer in *The Times* said: " Of the 9,000 English people who were in Switzerland in 1914 only a small proportion have so far returned to their familiar haunts, and their places have not been filled by visitors from other nations . . . with the end of the Swiss school holidays a silence has fallen. . . . The chant of cow bells falls through the forest with unfamiliar clearness on the once busy mule-paths and mountain roads; and the sprinkling of visitors take their pick of rooms in hotels where in other years they might have been grateful for a mattress in a bathroom."

Nobody realised how these European countries would be opened up like a tin of sardines by changes in transport . . . or that coaches would carry parties of tourists all over the continent. And least of all did the average person realise how his life was to be changed by the aeroplane. In 1919 the government had started the first regular air service to Paris. It began as a means of carrying members of the peace commission backwards and forwards for those talks at Versailles at the end of the war — talks which carried on for a long, long time. It wasn't long before aviation companies were formed, usually by young men who had served in the Royal Flying Corps during the war and now couldn't bear to give up flying. In 1919 the first "tourist" planes lumbered over to Paris. They were made, seemingly, of plywood, and were not very comfortable, holding about a dozen people who sat uncomfortably in cramped conditions. It was a horrifying experience, for the wings were very fragile and the engines were mounted under them. You had to be a brave holiday-maker to take to the air in those days. Aeroplanes seemed as slow and uncomfortable as the early cars, and a lot more dangerous. And as with the cars, most travellers thought they would never be used as everyday transport.

1. Osbert Sitwell "Laughter in the Next Room" Macmillan 1949

45

Holidays take to wheels.
"There's a little brown road winding over the hill . . ."

"The Bedpan" appeared in 1923. This unkind name was given to the first British baby car, intended for the masses. Its price, which seems low now, must have been rather steep for the average man at that time. The Austin Seven was £165. It wasn't the first small car, the Ford Tin Lizzie had already appeared and was even being put together in England; while all other cars offered a colour choice, the Ford came only in black. The large elegant cars of the past had often been much less reliable than these impudent little midgets which were supposedly used as ashtrays by drivers of bigger cars. There were lots of jokes about them . . . the young wife leaning from the bathroom window to say "I can't come down, I'm bathing baby" while a squat Morris Minor sits in the tub behind her; or the cartoon of the strong man picking

A charabanc outing, pre-1920s.

his "midget" up to stride through the traffic. But the baby car caught on, other small cars appeared and in a few years the roads to holiday resorts seemed to be packed bumper to bumper with tourists' cars.

They were a mixed blessing if you lived in the quiet villages of the West of England where the lanes were too narrow to hold anything more than a couple of cows abreast. In the days before restrictions on parking these incoming cars blocked people's gates, the pavements and every sideroad near the winding lanes of the coast. If you owned a tearoom or a gift shop (and there were more and more of these) of course you welcomed the motorist, he brought money into your business.

Hard behind the family car came the motor coach. 'Buses were originally used by passengers who wanted to get into the nearest town but as soon as they were mildly comfortable, they were used for longer journeys. In March 1923, the *Evening News* made a small feature of motor coach tours:

"The motor-coaching season promises to be more successful than ever this year.

"Many enquiries have already been made as to the programmes for the summer. For a start a six-day tour to the West of England has been arranged for Easter. Motor coaches will leave London on Thursday for Bournemouth, and on the following days Dorchester, Exeter, Torquay, Wells and Bath will be visited. The cost, including hotel charges, will be £9.9s."

Travellers could now expect to stay dry. It was only in the 1920s that charabancs and 'buses had covered tops, until then the very hardy who went on top in a double decker were wind-blown and rained upon. The open single decker 'bus presented the same problems.

Motor coaches (and their occupants) were thought to be noisy and common. They certainly came as a shock to those living in quiet villages which had hardly recovered from the arrival of the "baby" car. At least the car owners had some property even if it was all on four wheels and they could be expected to behave with some taste, thought the country people, but the "trippers", as motor coach travellers were called, hadn't even their respectability. They wanted, and got, cheaper food. They wanted, and got, public lavatories set up in beauty spots. They wanted entertainment and many seaside towns which had resisted funfairs and shooting galleries now had them opening on the promenade.

The motor coach tripper travelled in a big group and they rarely split up when they reached their holiday place. Many friendships, even marriages, were made on these tours. There was almost always a "funny man", and often, as there had been in the Edwardian days, a cornet or saxophone player who brought his instrument along for the ride. They brought children who were generally supposed to be less well behaved than the children who arrived by car. Pubs and cafes started to put up signs according to how they felt about the trippers:–"Coaches Welcome" or "No Coaches". The people who displayed the latter sign were thought to be snobs by coach passengers. The pub and cafe owners had different explanations. They thought that coach travellers would only buy a glass of beer or a cup of tea and that their noise would drive away the local people and those visitors who wanted spirits, the popular and expensive "cocktails" or proper meals. They were right too.

Along with complaints about the behaviour of coach parties in towns came worse moans about their activities in the country, for many coaches went to out-of-the-way beauty spots of woodland or seaside which hadn't been accessible before. Do you remember how the hop-pickers' children angered farmers by leaving gates open and running over crops? The farmers of the 1920s had those worries and others . . . litter. This had never been a problem before because few people were ever in one beautiful place at a time and if they did leave any paper bags lying about they were soon washed into the earth. Until the 'twenties only the rich had picnics, and they usually ate out of hampers leaving no debris. Soon many of the most at-

Bank Holiday fairground, 1925. Obviously posed!

tractive parts of the country were covered with empty sardine tins, beer bottles and fish and chip wrappers. There were even poems written about the new menace, in imitation of Shakespeare's songs:

> "Come unto these yellow sands
> And scream in bands;
> Picknicked when you have and flung
> The tins of tongue:
> Fling them wildly here and there
> Bottles that have held your beer.
> Scream! Squeal!
> Fling bun
> And scatter peel.
> What *fun*
> Hark! Hark! the clang
> Of homeward honking 'Cherrybang';
> Bank Holiday is done."

However the protestors might make out-cries like these, the coach tour operators continued to do well. Most of them only made trips for a day or an afternoon. In days when less traffic was on the road they could be out of the big cities and into the country very quickly. And they did make visits to the country possible for lots of people who either couldn't travel to the big stations for excursions, or who couldn't afford the higher railway fares. Besides, the easy get-together atmosphere of the coach trip suited parties from the same village or the same street who could collect enough neighbours and charter a coach themselves. The coaches, which were still called "charabancs", came to the end of the street and dropped their passengers back again at their own front doors late at night. The trippers from a community took their own funny hats and crates of beer and often cheated those cafés which catered for coaches by taking their own packed meals too.

In time all sorts of specialist groups began to arrange their own coach trips but the ones which were most common were fishing parties, which went off with their equipment in the early hours of the morning and would mournfully sit at the ends of those piers on which other holidaymakers enjoyed themselves. One-day trips were most common because it was a small number who could manage a week's holiday from home. Most working people still went away for the odd day and in the 1920s there were only 1½ million workers who had managed to have a week's holiday with pay in the year. Other workers had about half a dozen days off work but these were still special days like Christmas or Easter which were not necessarily spent away from home. There was still only one time of the year when many people went to the sea or the countryside and that was on August Bank Holiday.

Because of these short holidays, many boarding house keepers had found it better to supply bed and breakfast than the old fashioned seaside rooms with three meals a day. Poorer visitors, with only a short time to spare, wanted freedom during the day to arrange a cheaper system of eating or to go for trips to nearby towns or local places of interest. Rather unfairly these "bed and breakfast" houses were supposed to offer a low standard of comfort in order to save money, and better-off holiday makers avoided them. However, big houses on roads towards the sea started to have signs offering "Accommodation" in their windows and lots of amateur landladies went into business.

"Touring" was a new idea, only made possible by the motor car. Determined to see as much as possible of the Lake District or the Highlands of Scotland in the short time they had, motorists flitted about the countryside like bees visiting flowers and often saw very little except the roads.

They had good roads to drive on, although they were the cause of much bitterness, especially in areas where there were few cars belonging to local people, for the ratepayer kept up the roads and in return suffered the noise and smell of vehicles. In many areas, cars were still considered a menace and some villagers were capable of strewing their streets with broken glass in order to keep intruders out. It didn't help motorists that different local authorities had different speed limits for built-up areas, sometimes as low as ten or fifteen miles an hour and the local magistrates' courts were often packed on Monday mornings by drivers who had exceeded these low limits. Some magistrates were very hard on motorists from outside their own areas, Godalming was supposed to be particularly harsh — perhaps the magistrates suffered from living on a route to the South Coast.

Caravans were still thought an odd way to travel. After the war some homeless families had found refuge in abandoned or cheap railway carriages or old motor 'buses which were parked in fields, well away from the homes of more fortunate people. These camping sites very soon went downhill into the conditions which had been complained about for years on the gypsy camp sites. Living in poverty, with little water and no proper sewerage, the "caravans" became slummy and not surprisingly, most outsiders thought that a home on wheels was depressing and ugly.

However, in the 1920s some of the more arty people decided that gypsy caravans offered a pleasant way to relax on holiday. Caravans were then drawn by horses, not by cars, and this nostalgic memory of the old days suggested an escape from the noisy smelly journeys by motor. These rather artistic people blazed the way for all sorts of new ideas in the 1920s. Many of their notions seem rather pretentious and affected to us now, like their thoughts of "going back to the simple life" and "going back to the land" but as you will see in a later chapter, they were to

Hastings Beach in 1927.

49

A gypsy caravan and family. Such people were very common during the 1920's. (Liverpool University Library.)

alter middle class thoughts on holidays. As far as road travel went, they concentrated on the round wooden wheels of the gypsy vans. These vehicles were much smaller than motor caravans and less well ventilated. In fact when the stove was lit inside they became stuffy and dangerous because their varnished wooden sides were easily set on fire. Most of the people who hired them for holidays didn't cook in the van but outside on oil stoves perched on the grass.

Lavatories were usually nothing more than holes in the ground which were dug over. In those days all campers and caravaners took spades along with them! A lot of the "fun" of having a holiday in a gypsy caravan was supposed to be caring for the horse but as many of the visitors had always lived in towns and as the horses were large, most of the holiday was often spent chasing the animal in a vain attempt to catch it then harness it to the cart. Travelling was very slow and this was one of the attractions of the holiday, but at night there were often problems of finding a place

to park the van where the horse could also graze. While some farmers were amused by the "townsfolk" arriving in caravans which had always in the past been associated with thieves and beggars, many others saw no difference between gypsies and the artists who wore gaudy clothes and silk handkerchiefs knotted at their throats like the real "diddaki" people, so there were threats of dogs chasing the travellers down the road! Genuine gypsy caravans could always be seen at big race meetings like the Derby. Racegoers knew that the Romany caravans had rounded tops. Non-gypsy vans had flat roofs.

Here is an idea of the traffic at the old, pre-1914, Derby and the race in 1928. Caravans were still an important part of the scene but that they had been joined by other kinds of transport. The old donkey cart was on its way out and the only one or two horsedrawn coaches were still being run by rich men as an amusement. Karl Silex was writing about the English for Germans in his book *John Bull at*

A Showman's waggon with beautiful carving and painting. (Liverpool University Library.)

Home but it was translated back into English although it wasn't always very kind about our habits!

"Who would ever dare to describe the Derby? . . . People in England have time. Offices are all but closed. The head and his employees take the day off . . . On Tuesday evening the masses have already started on their migration to Epsom, and thousands spend the night in the open, and sleep in their cars or in tents. At seven o'clock on Wednesday morning the few roads leading from London to Epsom are packed with an unbroken chain of cars creeping at a snail's pace of about three quarters of a mile an hour towards the racecourse. Practical people make a detour of about a mile and reach the course without difficulty from the south. But what would the Derby be without traffic jams? So year after year people drive along

the same old crowded routes. The most ramshackle old vehicles are taken out of their sheds and stop dead in the middle of the road with their engines seized and their radiators seething, until one or two kindly policemen help to push them out of the way into a field or ditch. . . . About 60,000 cars are parked around the course and in the middle of the Epsom Downs. Like an army of tin soldiers 1,000 omnibuses draw up behind the cars, till the red citadel stands out like an impenetrable barrier from the Grand Stand to Tattenham Corner. The passengers all cluster on the top deck, while inside the conductor prepares lunch and tea. . . . A city of tents shelters the ever-popular sideshows of an English people's festival. The organs of the roundabouts try to drown each other in a Babel of sound, while there are also shooting ranges, dice-tables, lucky-wheels and

51

Ladies wear, 1928.

marionette theatres. . . . The crowds swing the hammer at the 'try-your-strength' machine and gather round the coconut shies to win coconuts. Gipsy women with dirty babies tell your fortune. In the beer tents the men drink their tepid bitter to the strains of a brass band. . . . Meanwhile the Pearly King may be seen strutting proudly with his family."

Race meetings were much more attractive to those with a "day off" in the 1920s than they would be today because many who couldn't afford a week's holiday could get into a different atmosphere for a few hours, and also because there was very little organised entertainment which explains why cinemas were so important in the lives of most of the public, and why the pub seemed the only place for many men to spend an evening. They were bored and needed somewhere to enjoy company at their leisure. It wasn't only the poor who got a thrill out of races. Rich people were even more closely in-

volved for they bred racehorses and owned them, and race meetings like Ascot were great social occasions on which the women would dress up and the men would saunter about comparing notes on the horses. They wore tailcoats and top hats and still do . . . Ascot Enclosure hasn't altered very much. There were enough wealthy people interested in the Grand National at Aintree for a new travel service to develop. In the late 1920s Imperial Airways had a special plane service from Croydon (near London) to Liverpool. It was a pity, thought some of the travellers, that they had to travel for an hour through the narrow streets of south London in order to reach the aerodrome. But at that time there was no London Airport except this rather small cramped airstrip. The Grand National visitors stayed in the cabins of the big ocean liners of Cunard which were moored at Liverpool. At night these liners were lit up with celebrating racegoers or those who wanted to forget how much they had lost at the National. Imperial Airways flew them back to London in time for the Boat Race. They would probably have guinea seats in the organised Grand Stand by the river from which they could watch the University boat teams row against each other. English "one day" holidays were still anchored to the great sporting occasions. Henley Regatta, which had been a great Edwardian raving event, felt rather hurt that George V never went to its boat races. Fewer visitors flocked down the Thames to gobble strawberries and cream when the Royal Family wasn't present.

Aeroplanes were still mysterious and rather dangerous and had little room for passengers. It was so expensive to take a plane up with only six or so passengers on board that only a very few could afford the fares. Many companies foundered in trying to cut prices and steal travellers from their rivals. The only regular British air services were between London and Paris or London and Le Touquet and these suffered because the French airways which competed with them had government grants and so could afford to cut their fare prices.

Ascot Enclosure, 1929. (Radio Times Hulton Picture Library.)

One of the first air services was Instone Airways, founded in 1920. They began a regular service to France in May and on their first flight went down low over Boulogne to scatter leaflets over the town, which must have been a surprise at a time when nobody expected anything to fall from the air except rain, sleet or snow. These advertisements offered single flights to Paris from London for ten guineas. A return was eighteen guineas, but . . . (and here the under-cutting comes in) . . . a return for *two* people was also eighteen guineas. Yet most people shook their heads; eighteen guineas was an awful lot of money, and flying was very risky.

Each plane carried ten people. In desperation the various air companies tried to advertise by releasing "news" stories to the papers, — that they flew mince pies to Paris for Christmas, or grapes from France to London. They also ran an air ambulance.

Right at the other end of the scale were most of the people who had very little means to go far away on holiday. Some of them didn't want to go on motor coach trips. The quieter "white collar" workers who wanted to "get away from it all" often had one week's holiday a year, especially if they worked for the Civil Service. Their great desire to get to the country, to find fresh air and to lead an open air life, often made many of them try too hard and spend their holidays exposing themselves to rain and wind on rambling or cycling holidays. They came back to their desks stiff, with streaming colds. Until the end of the 1920s there weren't many arrangements made for this sort of holiday-maker although soon after the war they were on their way, often in groups of about five or six together, cycling in long straggling lines along the quieter country roads. They wore shorts which were still rather extraordinary, and made the villagers stare. Most of the cyclists or walkers were fairly bookish, unadventurous people who were following the ideas of the "artistic" richer people who usually had friends or money to fall back on when they were stranded on a wet Sunday evening on the Yorkshire moors. We would feel sorry for these office workers, often wet through, ill-equipped for bad weather, unsure of their rights in trespassing, nervous of cows and horses, and with very little money. But they started a movement to get out into the country and to "do it yourself" which was to be followed by a lot of young holiday-makers in the years between the wars.

53

Do-it-yourself holidays.
"Paddling your own canoe . . ."

Hotels were not what they used to be . . . at least that was what writers in the 1920s and '30s thought. When the railways became the usual form of transport many inns had suffered, especially those along the main roads. Their custom had been taken by the Station Hotels and when the motor car was invented it suddenly awakened all the old posting houses left over from coaching days. Unlike the Sleeping Beauty they didn't seem as marvellous as they had been: "They had a strange notion that any man who owned a car must be rich" said one critic who was making a tour of England in order to recommend beauty spots to other car owners. They charged 7s. 6d. a night for a single room (37½p) and 6s. 6d. (32½p) for a dinner and, grumbled Thomas Burke, they didn't give value for money. "The landlords found that the sale of third rate goods at first rate prices was first rate business." Many travellers would not put up with inferior food and bad service ". . . a few people would not let well alone; and wanted to know why an institution which pretended to exist for the comfort of travellers could not to its job; why they had to pay West End chef prices for cooking somewhat inferior to that of a Good Pull Up for Carmen; why they had to take their turn with eight others for the morning bath; why they had to put up with, and pay heavily for, conditions which they would not have tolerated for one day in their own homes . . ." It was a sad state of affairs and it drove many

A customary round of golf.

holiday-makers away from the small hotels and boarding houses.

But not all of them. One of the oddities of people on holiday is that they will often pay for bad conditions because they always have done in the past. Between the wars many families went year after year to the same boarding house, and had a thoroughly uncomfortable time and came back for more. It was because they wanted to see the same old friends in the boarding house whom they had probably met on holiday in the first place, and because they knew the seaside town.

54

Usually the middle aged visitors felt this need to return each year, but the younger ones suffered because the normal seaside landlady could be very difficult over young children. Few wanted their guests to stay in if it rained, and in a week at the seaside one day was sure to be wet. At that time there were fewer amusements for families in seaside towns. More and more seaside towns realised that they would have to "cheapen" themselves and permit funfairs and indoor amusement arcades. In fine weather the beach offered enough pleasure for children with trips round the bay in rather smelly boats which would have been out collecting fish ten years before, and with Black and White Minstrels or Pierrots on the sand. The Pierrots were strange theatrical shows which only appeared at the seaside and they were in their heyday between the wars. Perhaps it was because so many young actors were out of work and found it pleasant to spend the summer by the sea and to earn a little money at the same time. The group was usually six or seven people with a pianist. The actors were almost

always young and attractive: "ingenues" as they were called at the time, although there was often an "uncle" figure who told jokes and did a "turn" intended to amuse the "kiddies" as Pierrots called the children who watched their show. They performed on a stage erected on the end of the pier or on the beach, with an awning over the stage but chairs on the sand or on the board floors of the pier for the audience.

The show was a series of short acts, some funny and some musical. Lots of light frivolous songs were sung to the accompaniment of the piano which faded in competition with the fresh air and sea wind. The costumes of the Pierrots were the most memorable thing about them. They wore floppy white smocks with big pompom black buttons down the front and hats like nightcaps. This was the traditional dress of the clown but they were not all clowns. Nearly everybody who remembers the Pierrots sees them as a period piece, their Noel Coward-type songs floating across the sand, their unfunny sketches falling flat with a critical

Ornamental Gardens, Clacton-on-Sea, 1929.

55

audience. Usually they were not very good, but they were as much part of a seaside holiday as the donkeys which paraded on the promenades and the Punch and Judy man. Lots of children hoped that when they grew up they would become Pierrots too, and sing on the beach.

Apart from more "Gifte Shoppes", tea-rooms and amusements arcades, the seaside had not altered a great deal since before the 1914-1918 war. The most important difference was that more people enjoyed it and in August the beaches were crowded. There were very few gaps between the buildings on the "prom", and in many towns the fishermen's cottages facing the sea had been pulled down and replaced by tall boarding houses.

There had always been a certain number of holiday makers who had avoided the sea in summer and had found other interests inland. Obviously those with children were bound to consider what they might like to do in the summer. There were inland waters. Arthur Ransome wrote his great series of books in the 1930s about the holidays of a group of children who had sailing adventures in the Lake District. The *Swallows and Amazons* were hardly ordinary children because although money was less of a worry in the 1920s than it had been before the war or would be in the '30s, very few children had their own sailing boats, or would have been allowed to camp and sail on their own all summer. But they were typical of some families who wanted to have "different" holidays. Children who liked riding were found rooms in a few farmhouses on Exmoor or Dartmoor where they could stay overnight and go on pony treks by day. These were not as organised as they were to be in our day. They were usually fixed up between friends. It was a sign that children were being considered as individuals with individual holiday tastes. Walking holidays which would have pleased grown ups were often too strenuous for young children.

In the 1920s it seemed that the whole population was on the move in the summer, and many of them on their own two feet. Hiking, as it was newly called, was the great outdoor sport of the period.

Many of these walkers came out for the day from the big cities. They were so numerous that London Transport published two guide books in 1923. These told hikers what attractions awaited them north and south of the city. They had maps showing them which way to go and were so popular that on many Sundays a seemingly never ending chain of ramblers walked behind each other in order to "get away" from the crowded city. Vicars were rather shocked that most of these walks took place on Sundays and so special services were devised for walkers in the beauty spots. The newspapers gave details of these and of interesting walks so that it was not surprising that the chosen places were overcrowded. Lots of walkers hoped to live in the country, but there was very little left in places near London. As the great roads spread out into the suburbs rows of houses streamed along them like pearls on a string. This was called "ribbon development" and it was increased by the opening of new Underground stations and the introduction of long distance 'buses. The countryside round big cities was being swallowed up and any ramblers who planned a day out had to go farther and farther away. Many ideas about hiking had come from Germany. The young Geman was a romantic figure in the 1920s and posters showed him in lederhosen (or short leather shorts) with the wind ruffling his blond hair and all his possessions tied up in a rucksack. Into the British rucksacks went all one needed for a ramble: chocolate bars, a waterproof, dry socks (very important), sticking plasters for blistered feet and a map. These were special "rambler's" maps which showed the tracks and rights of way across the countryside. Often farmers didn't agree with the maps and there were encounters with bulls, game-keepers and sticks, or barbed wire. But the hiker was a determined character. In Germany hostels had been set up where walkers could stay for the night. They were definitely not for car drivers, in fact most walkers thought of motorists with horror. *They* kept off the roads, and away from civilisation which many of them pretended to despise. By 1930 they had increased to such numbers that Youth Hostels were begun in England. These offered beds in dormitories and cooking facilities. Many young people had their first holidays by painfully walking from one Youth Hostels to another in the 1930s. This type of life emphasised the "get away" spirit but was often like grownups playing Boy Scouts, with campfire songs and suppers to which everybody contributed something so that you could end up with sardines-fried-egg-cucumber-and-currant buns. Cocoa was the usual drink.

Even the railways did well out of hikers. On Good Friday 1832 a Hikers' Express was sent out by the Great Western Railway. It carried walkers to an unknown destination from which they could ramble. They were returned, footsore, to Paddington in the evening. The idea was a tremendous success and the railway followed it with a "Kiddies Express". This took children, and only children, to Weston-super-Mare and clowns walked along the carriages to amuse the children on the journey.

Railway companies admitted that hikers did not compete with them but added to their profits; after all, one out-of-the-way "rail" hike, which had been expected to draw forty people, collected 1,440. More and more special trips were organised and soon Southern Region had regular hikers' excursion trains running at weekends. London, Midland and Scottish went further; they ran excursion trains for those who wanted to see beauty spots from the line. Special carriages were built with picture windows from which excursionists could see the beauties of the north. They ran especially slowly across the Yorkshire Dales. L.M.S. even ran a "Gretna Green Special" from the Lancashire towns to the village where romantic eloping couples had been married for centuries by Scottish law. Did hikers take advantage of this odd matrimonial agency? We don't know how many young couples eloped on the excursion

"GEOGRAPHIA"
Ramblers' Map
(Scale 1 inch to 1 Mile)

No. 5

COUNTRY ROUND
BOGNOR

FOOTPATHS &
BUS ROUTES
DISTINCTLY
INDICATED

Published 1/6 *by*
"GEOGRAPHIA" LTD
167 Fleet Street, London. E.C.4.

Ramblers' map cover, 1932.

special![2]

It's easy to find these hikers rather comical but they paved the way for more adventurous holidays in later years. In the Midlands and the North they were particularly popular and the Yorkshire Dales, the Pennines and Lake District were well explored. It was owing to the work of many of these hikers and ramblers that large parts of the countryside were appreciated for the first time, and became National Parks.

Some of the mountainous parts of Britain attracted rock climbers and potholers. Groups of young people, often with an appointed leader, would spend their weekends scrambling on the mountains or underneath them. We would think them foolhardy today as there was not the equipment for dealing with accidents that we know nowadays. There were few telephones in remote areas and if a climber fell he had little chance of getting to hospital quickly. Also many of the adventurers were amateurs, out for the first time. Like hikers they were usually office workers and took great chances without realising their own danger. A woman in her sixties describes potholing in the early 1930s: "It was good fun although I can see how dangerous it was now. We did some silly things. All I was told was to dress sensibly and bring a torch." "Sensible dress" was knickerbockers and rough knee socks or, in her case, a leather coat and beret worn with walking shoes. Every Saturday she went to potholes in a small Austin Seven and would spend the whole day underground, feeling her way along the wet rockwalls, and avoiding subterranean streams and pools. Occasionally the group would stop while the leader, who was able to reach a safe ledge in advance of the rest of them, took flashlight photographs.

The camera was a great aid to enjoying holidays. Showing your "snaps" became immensely important, a proof that you had a good time. The box Brownie had made photography cheap, and magazines fostered the new pleasure, with articles on catching childrens' smiles or making the most of the beach. Seaside resorts were stalking grounds for the beach photographer, a man who would dance ahead of visitors and click away at them, afterwards presenting a card with his name and address. Lots of holiday pictures survive which were taken this way and mounted, postcard size, on the back of a postcard so that the pictures could be sent to friends who were not lucky enough to be at the seaside.

July and August were traditionally poor periods in newspapers, when few world-shaking events happened, and many columns were filled with advice to holidaymakers, competitions for their "snaps" and challenge games when a girl dressed in pink tulle and wearing a feather hat or some such odd

Mundesley Beach, Norfolk, 1927.

A box brownie + a golf match = a hole in one?

these men felt defeated and hopeless as they met on street corners for a "gasper" and talked over their own misery. Or, if they lived in London, they could have gone hop picking. Hop picking holidays were still miserable. George Orwell left an account of one in his novel *A Clergyman's Daugher*: The pickers managed to sing while they picked and their hands were stained black with sulphur, while small hop lice crept into the pickers' hair. They sang in unison, usually popsongs which they knew from the radio . . . or wireless as the brown Bakelite set was called in the 1930s.

"The rate of pay at Cairn's was twopence a bushel, and given good hops a practised picker can average three bushels an hour . . . it would have been possible to earn thirty shillings (£1.50) for a sixty hour week. Actually no one in the camp came anywhere near this figure. The best pickers of all earned thirteen or fourteen shillings a week, and the worst hardly as much as six shillings . . ."

They earned so little because of the hours they "wasted". There were times when the hop bins had to be carried onto the next field which might be a mile away. And it rained; in this year, one day in three was wet and the pickers could do nothing except shelter under the hop plants, or bines, with sacks over their shoulders. When the sun came out the hops were wet and slippery and had dwindled in the rain. One of the worst problems in hop picking, according to Orwell, was that the pickers hardly ever had proper meals. They were exhausted when they came back from the fields and they had such poor cooking conditions that they would exist on bread, tea and bacon. They were hardly ever clean either, for the hop juice stained their hands and faces and their washing was done in a stream. It was all very dispiriting.

"This did not matter to the majority of the pickers, for quite half of them were gypsies and accustomed to starvation wages and most of the others were respectable East Enders, costermongers and small shopkeepers and the like, who came hop-picking for a holiday and were satisfied if they

costume could be "spotted" by readers who would win tickets for the local seaside show or free copies of the newspaper for a year. Occasionally prizes were more valuable. Reading the newspapers of the 1930s one imagines the whole population on holiday and the sun always shining. In fact the Depression was settling into people's lives like a terrible disease. There were many unemployed and some families were very near starvation. But in general they were the unskilled workers, unable to afford holidays anyway at the best of times, and so the crowds which packed the beaches were often oblivious to the poverty and tragedy of the people in the big industrial towns.

You could say that the unemployed were enjoying an everlasting holiday but the real problem of being out of work was not only that you didn't eat properly and couldn't replace your shoes when they wore out, but also that you lost the will to work. Some young men didn't have jobs from the time they left school until the war in 1939 provided them ironically with work, and earned enough for their fare both ways and a bit of fun on Saturday nights. The farmers knew this and traded on it. Indeed, were it not that hop-picking is regarded as a holiday, the industry would collapse . . ."

But Dorothy and Nobby, who were picking for money in order to live, found that they could hardly manage on one and sixpence a day for the two of them. ". . . The local shopkeepers with four hundred hop pickers quartered upon them made more during the hop season than all the rest of the year put together . . . In the afternoon the farm hands would come round the bins selling apples and pears at seven a penny, and London hawkers would come with baskets of dougnuts or water ices or "halfpenny lollies . . ."

On Sundays the hop pickers didn't work, they needed the day to recover and to cook their main meal of the week. A Mission to hop pickers (remember the Missions in the East End of London?) held outdoor services. Mothers did their families' washing in great vats of water boiled on top of wood fires. The faggots of wood were provided by the farmer for whom they worked. What attracted the Londoners to these sad fields of hops where they worked so hard and earned so little? "You went home . . . swearing that you would never go hopping again . . . until next August, when you had forgotten the cold nights and the bad pay and the damage to your hands, and remembered only the blow-sy afternoons in the sun and the boozing of stone pots of beer round the red camp fires at night."[1]

Even the poorest had been seized with a fever for out of doors and freedom from town life. Children of better-off families were

Farm workers haymaking, 1934. (University of Leeds.)

Boy Scouts with a trek cart. (Scout Association.)

encouraged to love the country by camping
with Scout or Guide troupes. From its beginning by Baden Powell, a hero of the Boer
War, this enterprise had caught on like
measles. Joining a group which wore a
uniform was the ambition of every boy in
those days. It was important that you
belonged, that you learnt all this peculiar lore
of tracking and erecting tents and lighting
fires without matches. Many boys couldn't
afford the khaki tunic, shorts and slouch hat
and wore strange mixtures of uniform. The
scouting movement was important because it
took boys out of their homes and away from
towns. Nowadays schools organise group
outings and holidays and many boys go camping, but in the 1920s and '30s it was a new
idea for children to get away on their own.
Other organisations ran holiday camping
weeks, many with church associations, but
none were to be as well known as the Boy
Scout Movement.

Almost as soon as a Boy Scout joined the
movement he wanted to be off and away.
There seemed little point in learning about
tracking and living off the land if you were
cooped up in city streets, especially in
Glasgow, the big industrial centres of the
north, or the East End of London. Although
scouting was perhaps most popular in the
south east of England, its followers made off
for the fells and dales in their own parts of the
country. London scouts tended to go to Ep-
ping Forest. One of the first things a new
scout troop opted for was a trek cart which
could take all their gear when they walked (no
nonsense about going by train or 'bus!) to
their camping site. They might very well buy
an old coster's barrow or builder's cart,
precariously poised on two wheels, for a

61

pound or so, and would refurbish it themselves . . . after all some of them aimed for woodworker's badges. A troop of about a dozen or so boys and their scout master, who was very often a teacher at school, would share a big bell tent which was one of the most difficult to put up, suspended from a central pole with great need for tautness in the ropes which anchored it to the ground. By 1930 some troops had a groundsheet so the scouts didn't sleep on the bare earth although many of them had hoped to hollow a hole for their hips and sleep "really rough" as Indian scouts did in the Canadian backwoods. To us, their equipment would seem fairly rough anyway. Of course they had no camp beds and slept in very primitive sleeping bags. The luxurious kapok or Terylene filled bags were not known yet and so the boys made do with blankets brought from home, either folded in such a way that they couldn't come undone (if they were good scouts) or, very often, pinned with enormous safety pins also brought from home. In spite of their preference for living off the land many boys loved the tinned luxuries of the '30s too much to go without them, and lived on condensed milk, "bully" beef and baked beans. But they did cook in mess tins like soldiers. They usually camped on common ground, in places which were open to the public like the big forests or hill districts where the local inhabitants were by now used to campers and ramblers. The Boy Scouts were often more welcome than their elders for they were carefully coached in closing gates and running silently along the edges of fields. Many farmers must have smiled when they saw a scout troop appear on their land, with wideawake hats and long staffs, and at their belts the dreaded Scouting knife which would be considered a weapon by the police today. These knives were part of the delight of boyhood, with clasps for opening tins, cutting branches and removing stones from horses' hooves.

The hikers of Great Britain had identified themselves very often with the German "Wandervögel" or youth movement but they

might have responded more kindly to the ingenious boy scout who was younger, more enthusiastic, and in spite of the uniform, and the hierarchy of leaders — brown owls and chief scouts — less regimented than the youth movements of Germany; "he (the Englishman) imagines men wandering over forest and fen as irresponsibly as the birds their namesakes; strolling hither and thither as the spirit moves them, sharing pot luck and finding shelter in barns". In fact, revealed a writer in 1931, the Wandervögel were highly organised and efficient, and not at all like the boy scouts who carried their own efficiency with the lopsided ease of their cocked bush hats.

Other semi-military organisations also had "jamborees" especially the Territorial Army which became quite important in the 1930s. Some commentators felt it was alarming to have ordinary men gathering to drill and play at soliders in peace time but the "terriers" enjoyed themselves and most of all, delighted in the week in camp which they had once a year, acting like real soldiers, and far away from the drudgery of family life. They thought of their week under canvas as a holiday when they could shed their roles as bank clerks and shop assistants. Many of them were very useful when war actually did break out. You will notice from the type of people who joined the Terriers that camping was most popular with so called "white collar" workers, men who didn't have to dirty their hands during the rest of the year and it's not surprising that living in this way appealed most to those who had a certain amount of luxury during their everyday working life. Hot water, a bath, and a comfortable bed were not so common in the 1920s and '30s. Many people still had a scrub in a tin bath before an open fire. Obviously those who enjoyed woodfires and testing guyropes were those who found it all an adventure. They were also the ones who could afford to get away from home.

Scouts were usually fairly well off too. We wouldn't think so today when we know how they made-do-and-mended to buy a cart, a tent, and their familiar uniforms, but they came from the "respectable" families who had roast meat and rice pudding for Sunday lunch . . . or dinner as it was called commonly then, Poorer children were still traipsing the cities with their small brothers and sisters, getting up to mischief in the street markets and parks. Smart organisations like the Scouts appealed to them no more than the Territorial Army appealed to their fathers and older brothers.

Many of these children had even less chance of a holiday than their parents had when they were children. The Missions and church outings were less common because churches and chapels were less well attended. People who were better off "went for a drive" on Sundays in their little cars, and those who were less well off thought very often that church was a conspiracy of the middle classes and felt they had lost their religious faith in the First World War. So the treats and picnics which the church had arranged before 1914 had often disappeared from lack of support. If there were no children, there were no days by the sea or in the country.

In the 1930s quite a few books were written for children which told them how to spend their leisure time. They weren't dull or patronising and probably the best of them was *The Holiday Book* by Clough Williams-Ellis which was illustrated by one of his daughters. They gave instructions on flower-collecting and pressing, camping, sailing, basic cookery and indoor games for wet weather. They have lasted very well, but one odd thing about them strikes us today. They were intended for fairly well-off children, which was to be expected as *their* parents would buy the book, and they suggested that children of this type would have country cottages.

Until the 1920s and '30s only the very rich had two homes and they had moved from one to the other very ponderously, like tortoises, by way of wagonette or brougham to the nearest station which might be twenty miles away, then to London and then by cab to their town houses. They didn't live in flats. Some big blocks of flats had been built in London at the turn of the century but the very rich had houses in Mayfair and Belgravia, or

Getting away from it all on a boat.

if they were not so well off, Kensington. Having made this great journey they then had to stay either in the country or the town for a month or so to make the trip worthwhile, and out of this slow calendar of moving from town to country and back again, had come the London Season when "anybody who was anybody" was in London for several months. The Season was still operating in the 1920s and '30s but the travel was more whirlwind. Both the very rich and the well-off middle classes had been set free by the motor car. Professional men earning around £1,000 a year could very well afford a second home. At the same time there was this craze for "getting back to the land" and "finding grass roots" and the two welded together so that the Londoners descended on out-of-the-way villages, bought cottages, did them up and led two lives. During the week they were doctors or university lecturers or businessmen in town, wearing pinstriped suits and bowler hats or toppers. On Friday evening they clambered into their fast cars

and went into the country, so that by Saturday morning they were dressed in old shirts and shabby corduroys or flannel bags, and trimming the hedges round their quaint country homes. Most Londoners looked for the type of thatched cottage we see on birthday cards. They had crazy paving paths, wells, and beams which knocked your head when you went in by the front door. Londoners brought water into the houses, built lavatories and summerhouses and prepared to make them their holiday homes. They caused great joking when they arrived, but by-and-by the local villagers accepted them, and allowed them to drink in their local pub without being standoffish, and even made a bit of money out of the newcomers. After all, they were employed as gardeners, household helps and builders and decorators so they did quite well out of the Country Cottage Craze.

When one cottage in a village was done up, and another became vacant, it was usually sold to Londoners too. They followed each other like swarming bees and soon whole

The 'ideal' country cottage.

colonies of weekenders would take over small villages in Sussex, Hampshire or the Cotswolds. Few of them went from London to Wales or the Lake District, cars were not capable of such strenuous journeys then, but these areas had their own "weekenders" who came from Birmingham, Manchester, Liverpool or Leeds.

The cottages were bought for very small sums, sometimes as little as £80 each. In those days that was probably a fair price for them, for they had been allowed to become almost derelict and town people spent a lot of money doing them up and making them comfortable. The villages were altered from Friday to Monday, instead of silent streets where a few carthorses caused a diversion, they were bright with young people with gaudy clothes and high voices who bought their groceries at the village shop, joined the cricket team and had parties for other Londoners which kept the village awake until midnight. Many of the visitors were people who had no regular working hours and so ac-

tors, writers and painters congregated together on each others' lawns for Sunday morning drinks, watched with amazement by the villagers.

Many books were written on the theme of "how we found and did up our little country home" and the writers were often very patronising about the villagers, giving them dialect accents and making them seem ridiculous. Fortunately few of their real country neighbours ever read these books so they weren't hurt by them. And in those days country people *were* often more slow than those of the town, they didn't have the same education and they didn't have the same interests.

Inevitably children came with the Londoners. They hardly ever played with the village children but with their friends from similar families. It was as if they spoke a different language from the country children. But they did learn about the countryside on those weekends in it, and they probably found much more in village life than their

Isolated but select; country living.

parents who were always ready to rush back to town if there was a party in Chelsea or if the water pipes froze in the cottages. In some ways having a country cottage was a mistake for the children too, because although most of them grew to love their second homes, they cut down on their chances of going to different places for holidays, or going abroad. A few of them did become a bit bored with their thatched homes, but their parents didn't, they were surrounded by their own friends.

One good result of the system was that many of these part-time country children stayed in the villages when they grew up, having learnt to enjoy them better than towns, and of course a lot of cottages were saved which might have fallen down, for country people were going to live in towns where there was more work. They changed places with the rich townspeople.

Some of the authorities in resort towns had realised that if they were not to be left behind in the profitable work of providing holidays, and if they did not want to become "common" with amusement arcades, they would have to open something extra, which would attract what they thought of as the "right" visitors and which would keep the boarding houses and hotels packed from May until September. A few resorts decided that sailing was the answer. There was not the great interest that would come after the second world war, for boats were quite expensive and usually you had to grow up by the sea not to be afraid of it. However, some places developed as sailing centres . . . Burnham on Crouch which was near to London, Bosham, and the estuaries of Cornwall and Devon. These last were of most interest to local people or those who had retired, for Londoners couldn't reach the places for odd weekends. Those who wanted to be on the water but who didn't have a tempestuous link with the sea, could stay in the houseboat colonies which grew up along the Thames. These began as part-time homes rather like country cottages but later would be used as

Town children off to the country.

66

permanent homes. The Norfolk Broads were still of most interest to those visitors who wished to study wildlife. Barges had as yet hardly been used for holidays. They, and narrow boats, were still rather old-fashioned working vessels, used to carry coal and china clay from one part of the country to another. The whole cult of barge life was known only to a few devotees.

The alternative to establishing a sailing centre was to make a golf course and many seaside towns very shrewdly developed courses in the 1920s and '30s when land was still comparatively cheap and before the great interest in golf in the 1960s. This doesn't mean that golf was not popular. It had been established by the Prince of Wales (later Duke of Windsor): "The Royal Captain, wearing Highland dress, arrived in St. Andrews from Balmoral on 26th September, 1922 . . . Next morning some seven thousand people watched through the mist while Andrew Kirkaldy . . . teed up the royal ball, and, when the Prince exclaimed 'This is an awful job', replied 'Keep your eye on the ball!'."

Golf became an English passion from being a quaint Scottish traditional game. It was an expensive passion even then, for clubs cost a lot and the extras connected with golf were very dear, not only paying for a caddy, or boy to carry your bag, but also for rounds of drinks in the clubhouse after a game. One of the attractions may even have been the dress connected with golf which had been made fashionable by the Prince of Wales. These suits were of plus-fours, or baggy knickerbockers in rough Harris tweed which were tucked into calf-high socks. Worn with a flat golfing cap they "wowed" the ladies, for men had few chances to show off their elegantly turned legs. Many men who never went near a golf course paid a great deal for plus-four suits, to the indignation of true golfers. If the father of a family played golf his wife and children would find that they spent every holiday in a resort with a golf course. Golf was an odd interest because it emerged so definitely in the 1920s but those who rode, or climbed mountains or did underwater swim-

ming for pleasure had always been able to contrive holidays which incorporated their spare time hobby.

Until after the Second World War many people would not have had any chance to follow their odd pursuits, so although a few holidaymakers managed to scramble up Ben Nevis or watch wildfowl in the Fens there were no organised centres for them, and little effort made to establish training places or hostels. They were probably more happy to be overlooked by the holiday industry which might spoil their quiet dedicated interests.

1. George Orwell: *A Clergyman's Daughter.* Gollancz 1935.
2. Robert Graves and Alan Hodge: *The Long Weekend.* Faber 1941.

Golfing mania, joke card.

Going abroad.
"The last time I saw Paris . . ."

The Graf Zeppelin. (Radio Times Hulton Picture Library.)

Many people didn't count any time away from home as a holiday unless it was spent abroad. Aeroplanes were still lashed together with piano wire in the early '20s, and held 16 people ranged down each side of the cabin on wooden seats. The exposed engines were under each wing. In the 1920s you opted for a more comfortable mode of travel, and most of the voyagers still went in the Victorian way, by boat.

One of the most revolutionary attempts to carry passengers abroad was by airship. After 1918 the Germans had developed immense airships like the Graf Zeppelin. These were enormous silver balloons filled with gas which looked like cigars floating through the sky. A huge cabin was suspended from the balloon. Airships were not short of space, and the bedrooms were palatial. The dining rooms and lounges were like those of large hotels. The R34 was a British airship which made a Trans-Atlantic flight in 1919, and partly because the Germans were going so far ahead with *their* plans the British determined to have a bigger and better airship than anybody else. They were right in realising that whoever produced air transport which could carry hundreds of people at a time would make a lot of money, but hardly anybody except a few pioneers guessed that large airliners would develop from the tiny bi-planes of the 1920s.

In the early 1930s work started on a monster airship called the R 101. The air minister, Lord Thomson, said it would be "safe as houses except for a millionth of a chance". An inaugural flight was fixed in October 1934, when the airship would carry a few privileged passengers to India. The R101 was hardly ready in time and was completed

The Graf Zeppelin over England, 1930. (Radio Times Hulton Picture Library.)

The R.101 at the mooring mast Cardington, Bedford. (Radio Times Hulton Picture Library.)

almost immediately before it was due to take flight. It was finally finished off so quickly that it had no certificate of airworthiness. Its triumphant inaugural flight would also be its test flight. The aircrew were very apprehensive. They were also very tired for they had no rest between learning how to fly the airship and actually taking it up for its journey to India. It mounted in the sky with a crew and six passengers on board, one of whom was Lord Thomson. It took $1\frac{1}{2}$ hours to travel the first fifty miles and the passengers decided to go to bed when the R 101 crossed the French coast at 11.26 p.m. It was obviously going to be a leisurely voyage. At 2.08 a.m. the R 101 crashed near Beauvais in Northern France. The gas flared into a monstrous fire and miraculously six people were pulled out from the blaze. But it had terrified the public who were to be wary of airflight for some time afterwards. They preferred a comparatively safe and well tried method of going from one country to another.

Few holidaymakers travelled abroad by car because there were no motor carriers across the Channel although they could hire cars on the Continent. If you were very smart you went to France by the Golden Arrow. The famous train had been constructed because of the popularity of the South of France. The British somehow managed to keep the resorts of Cannes, Nice and Juan les Pins as British preserves. Few French went to the Riviera, — perhaps because they found it expensive, and also it seemed farther than London from Paris. This was due to the magic of the Golden Arrow which travelled from Victoria to Dover, put its passengers on a ferry boat and was superseded by another Golden Arrow train in France which went down to the coast. In France it was "La Flèche d'Or". From the beginning the train was meant to be exclusive. It had only been possible as a project because several railway companies in the south of England were combined after the Railways Act of 1923 which put the running of railway lines into a few hands. By joining the rolling stock and standardising the mechanism, a more competent railway service was possible ... and more money could be invested in ideas like the Golden Arrow.

The train was a success from the first day it ran in 1929. It had "Limited Service", that is, only the same number of tickets were sold as there were seats. Its six Pullman coaches carried three hundred privileged people. The extent of their privilege was seen at Dover when the Golden Arrow passengers bypassed the regular customs services, going into a special section so that they would not be delayed and hold up the sailing of the Golden Arrow ship, "The Canterbury". Two years later the Golden Arrow had its first setback when the autocarrier was introduced, a cross-Channel ferry which carried cars. And yet the magic of the luxury train still carried over until the 1939 war. It was a mark of status to say: "I'm going by Golden Arrow". Wagons Lits attached their coaches to the main train. They had remained as subdued and elegant as they had been before 1914 when they had carried passengers across Europe. The great trains which were almost legends like the Orient Express, had Wagons Lits (or sleeping cars) hitched onto them at the ports so that passengers travelled across Europe in their own bedrooms. Lined with deep gleaming wooden panels, their plushy travelling rugs immaculately folded by the attendant, they each had a tip-up wash basin and small wardrobe. Bunks were arranged above each other with a small ladder leading to the upper berth. The other fitments were, and still are, of knotted velvet, including a fob on which a watch could be hung.

These intimate little cabins voyaged across Europe at night while their occupants slept soundly, waking in Beirut, or Russia or the South of France. As a means of transport they were perhaps the only way in which the sensation of travelling by coach was preserved, with each voyager secure in his own little room. They were an adventure for children for they had the exotic atmosphere of cabins in Edwardian ships, and the bunks were a delight.

Most of this extravagant travel was directed towards the sun. This was largely because attitudes towards sunshine had altered since the days of the Edwardians. Sunlight had then been loathsome, it gave girls freckles and dyed their skins an ugly brown colour, and so sunshades had been used during the summer months and any young ladies who had to stay on the beach wore floppy wide brimmed hats. But in the early 1920s doctors discovered that sunshine actually helped to make weak children healthy and promoted the idea that instead of damaging the skin, sunlight might make you stronger and more resistant to illness.

It was 1928 when sunbathing became really popular owing to a phenomenally hot summer. It was also later to add something to the cult for nudity. At first nudists were treated as a joke. They came of the same ranks as vegetarians and the few people who wanted entirely to grow their own food or to weave their own fabrics. Their idea was that by taking off your clothes you became more free in your attitude to life as well as in your body. Germany led the way as it had with hiking. In the early 1930s an English woman writer was shocked when she visited a young peoples' camp in Germany and saw girls wearing nothing above their hips. At first English nudists met in each others' gardens if they were well screened, or in rather prickly woodland. However, as most of the followers of nudity were quite well off, they soon had enough money to build nature camps which were in fact the first holiday camps, with cabins for guests, a communal dining room (often serving vegetarian food), and social meetings at which everybody pretended not to notice that the others were naked. Soon nudity died out, mainly because of the climate, and also perhaps because the camps were rather boring. However, by the time they had become less popular the ideas of nudism and sunbathing had resulted in scantier swimsuits. Still one piece, they now had daring low backs although the men still had some covering on the upper part of their bodies. In an attempt to make swimsuits

A group of nudists, 1930. (Health & Efficiency.)

more revealing there was even a fashion for costumes with deep holes under the arms which looked moth-eaten. Women wore trousers on the beach. They were part of a two-piece suit called lounging pyjamas and were very full from the hips so that they looked more like a wide divided skirt than trousers. They were made of very soft fabrics like crêpe de chine and only worn by the Bright Young Things. This odd name was given to people who went to parties by pram dressed as overgrown babies, drank in nightclubs, and then went off on . . . what else? . . . the Golden Arrow to the wicked South of France. Hardly any of them seemed to have any work to do but they reminded the rest of Britain that there was some gaiety in the most difficult years of the Depression although they were criticised, often very rightly. A few of the girls were "artists". Painting was almost a fashionable sport among

young ladies of the 1930s. It gave girls from wealthy families a chance to break away from home and set up with another girl in a flat in Chelsea where they had lengthy holidays pretending to work.

Those who did get away to the Riviera aped the Bright Young Things written about by clever writers like Michael Arlen and Noel Coward, visiting each other in the flatfronted white villas which had mushroomed along the Mediterranean coast, drinking cocktails with unlikely names and dancing on the open air terraces. In one of Arlen's short stories *The Lost Generation*, he describes life in one of these villas seen by a practical forty year old engineer called Hemingway: "The life delighted him. They bathed all day from Beulah's small yacht which was anchored in the incredibly bright sandy-bottomed stretch between the two islands that lie a mile or so off the bay of Cannes. They did not go near

The Bathing Pool, Gt. Yarmouth, 1930. Note the swimming costumes.

Blankenberg, Belgium in the 1930s.

Cap d'Antibes or the Casino in Juan-les-Pins which were 'smart' and therefore not on Beulah's lawful occasions. Beulah had a speedboat too, which was not going too well on Hemingway's arrival . . . he found himself to his surprise holding the attention of young people. Yes, he felt they welcomed him. Sprawling about the deck in the skimpiest bathing costumes, saturated with salt and sunlight, Hemingway found peace."

However, Arlen's picture of the Riviera dominated by simple pleasures in the sun was very different from that of the gossip writers. Newspaper columnists followed the noisy extravagant crowds, writing about their adventures for readers. Venice was another centre for high living. The Lido had been created as a holiday centre for the rich: "The day's programme at the Lido is not strenuous: there are tennis courts though except when the tournament is in progress, I have rarely seen them used . . .

"Bathing in the sea and in the sun occupies

the morning assisted by eating the lovely fresh green figs (locally grown) . . . After a light luncheon there are bridge, backgammon and more sunbathing on the beach; towards five o'clock people return to dress, preparatory to going to Venice for the evening."

Occasionally the smart visitors ventured off the coasts of Italy and France to explore their interior, they mounted from the Riviera by way of the Corniche roads, on twisting hairpin bends mounting into the hills which taxed the cars and drivers of that day: "The Grand Corniche is now a road devoted to the seeker after pleasure", wrote Sir Frederick Treves in 1921. "People traverse it, not with the object of arriving at any particular destination, but for the delight of the road itself, of the joy it gives to the eye and the imagination. Its only traffic is what transport agents would call 'holiday traffic'; for when the idle season ends the highway is deserted."

Sir Frederick found British influences

BREEDENE-sur-MER — Les Bains.

Holidays in Northern France: Breedene-sur-Mer, 1932.

everywhere, especially on the Monte Carlo golf course where the caddies spoke a kind of pidgin English. The Monaco dog show seemed different from any other though it was largely patronised by permanent British residents.

"It is held on the Terrace and is unique of its kind. It is not really a dog show but rather a dogs' afternoon party, where dogs of both sexes meet, renew acquaintances, gossip after their fashion with much tail wagging . . . There are no stands upon which the dogs are staged, no kennels, no baskets with rugs . . . There are no placards, no cards, no advertisements of dog biscuits . . . The dog owners (mostly ladies) are dressed in their very best . . . At intervals a man with a megaphone shouts from the bandstand the names of certain dog owners . . ."

There were also earnest visitors to France who wanted to see the ruins and to walk about the countryside, for rambling had penetrated here as well. *Off the Beaten Track in Southern France* was written in 1928, and in it Roy Elston suggests walking trips and also tells us what to expect to pay. He did not go to very fashionable places but proposed that the average tourist should travel first class by train and autocar ('bus to us). He calculated that a three week holiday would cost about £20. The first class return fare across the Channel was £6 5s. 7d. (just over £6.25). You would pay 80 francs for a 'bus seat from Paris to the South. He says: "The expense of such a trip would be negligible. If you allow yourself five shillings (25p) a day you will find it sufficient. This as a twelve hour day trip would cost something between three and four pounds sterling. The hotels, for our standards are ridiculously cheap (remember this is inland from the Riviera) . . . and the meals they supply are always good and sometimes excellent. But don't ask for English foods, rosbif and that sort of thing. The French will never know how to cook that sort of thing".

Mr Elston did add notes for the motorist, although he pleads that he is not one himself, and a list of extras that a car driver should take with him. A collapsible canvas water bucket and a complete set of spare globes are included. In some areas he warns that there are few garages and he adds that spare parts may be unobtainable, especially for British cars.

Italy and Germany were very popular, indeed many young Englishmen went to live in Germany after they left university in the early '30s, eking out a living by giving lessons and writing for magazines in London. They were almost all impressed by the new qualities in Germany, its cleanliness, its "get up and go" spirit, although just a few, like Christopher Isherwood, saw that the regimented young people who went on camping holidays in the woods and mountains might also turn into a danger; at least, a danger to Germany. Few guessed that they would be a menace to the rest of Europe. One reason for the popularity

Advertisement for a holiday in Budapest, Hungary, 1938.

of trips to Germany was its cheapness, for owing to the fall in value of the mark you could have a very cheap holiday by the Rhine. So cheap that many people thought of going abroad who would have considered it beyond them a few years before.

The few travel agencies in existence began to promote the package deal holiday which almost at once became popular. Holidays in the less fashionable resorts on the Riviera cost £8 for ten days, and in Germany cost about £12 for a fortnight. Young typists and clerks saved all year for these pleasures, and remember that going abroad was a real adventure in those days. Few of their families had ever been overseas except in the war, languages were not taught in ordinary schools and only a few years before a holiday of any kind would have seemed an impossible dream for many of the young people who

hurried to the Continent in the 1930s.

The earliest package deal holidaymakers were usually sent off by train, for although motor coaches had become comparatively luxurious by the early 1930s they were still uncomfortable compared with trains, and as the main "autoroute" system had not been built in Europe 'buses were much slower than trains. Travel by train meant that the tourist would not have to pay for a hotel on the way. Few of the new style holidaymakers would take advantage of the expensive and comfortable wagons lits. They took with them, or had provided by the agency, a blanket and a pillow and with these they made their beds, crouching in the corner seats of the railway carriage. Looking back, many of the tourists now feel they were very hard done by but admit that the holidays were very cheap . . . and then they were usual-

£ now buys over 21 Swiss francs

Photo: Aschwanden

Central Switzerland Lake Lucerne

A typical holiday advertisement for Switzerland, sounding very attractive.

ly very young. The change of customer also altered the places they visited. The richer and more snobbish British visitors complained that the Riviera was "quite spoilt" by package deal tourists although the very, very rich did not think so and continued the retreat to their villas in the summer. They had managed to buy property on the coast before the popular hotels were built and so they were able to surround their villas with large gardens filled with cypress trees, and with boundaries of high walls, so that the new-comers could not see into their private worlds. Some of the houses in places like Cap d'Antibes also had beaches of their own which were inaccessible from the land and on which could be landed the speed boats which had become a nuisance to sailors in Britain as well as the South of France. Small, noisy and fast, the quickly circling speedboat seemed a sign of the times to older holiday-makers who were disturbed by it. What was more surprising was the uses to which it was put, towing men and women at a new sport . . .

water-skiing. Yes, many people shook their heads at the way in which the Riviera was changing . . . cheaper nightclubs, cheaper restaurants, motorcoaches parked in the main squares, and children paddling from the public beaches. They resolved to go elsewhere and new notions of holidays evolved out of their desire to get away from the crowd . . . from a crowd they did not know that is, for the "smart set" still tended to travel in groups as they had in the days of Edward VII. To provide them with alternative holidays, resorts were opened in the West Indies, or in North Africa and America and the Big Game Safari was devised as a new way to pass the time.

In after years these places and diversions would also be overtaken by the package deal holiday agencies but they would remain expensive enough to discourage the crowds who travelled in motorcoaches and lived cheaply.

One of the most popular rich peoples' package deals was a trip to Egypt. In 1923 the

Cairo, a popular centre for tourists in Egypt during the 1920s.

77

Tourists visiting the Sphinx and Pyramids in Egypt. (Radio Times Hulton Picture Library.)

tomb of Tutankhamen was discovered at Luxor and there had been a spate of interest in everything to do with Ancient Egypt. At first the visit to the Pharaoh's tombs had been made privately and at some expense, but by the 1930s Thomas Cook's were sending parties across the sands to photograph the sphinx by moonlight.

Curiously, there were some countries which might seem to have more obvious pleasures than North Africa, yet did not attract many visitors. Spain was to be unknown to the general public until long after the Second World War. Little fishing villages where the local inn was a hovel with a mud floor, a diet of stringy meat, and an unattractive landscape ... that's how the mass of British people saw Spain. The few who did go there were adventurers, like young Laurie Lee, the poet who set off at the age of seventeen, penniless, hoping to work his way round the country of which he knew little more than the name. The writer Ernest Hemingway gave it some publicity but generally Spain was almost disregarded until the civil war broke out in July 1936. For some Englishmen their first sight of a foreign country was Spain in that year when they went to join the International Brigade, a group of foreign anti-Fascist soldiers who went to the aid of Spanish communists. It was hardly a holiday, but it showed how attitudes in Britain were changing to "abroad". Europe was suddenly near, and crossing to Spain was like walking over a doorstep.

Countries like Greece still seemed as remote and forbidding as Peru would be today. With no tourists, the countries to the east of the Mediterranean were screened from influences of more "civilised" lands. Their people were still peasants who lived very poorly, they relied on fishing and farming for a livelihood. Robert Byron was a young Englishman who went to Greece in 1925. It was an unusual holiday and he went prepared for rough living: "At 10.51 on Friday August 12th, I left Victoria, surrounded by a suitcase, kitbag, saddle bags, hat box (harbouring, besides a panama, towels and pillowcases), syphon box and a smug despatch-case that contained an Edgar Wallace (thriller) and credentials to every grade of foreign dignitary, from the Customs to the higher clergy". He made the second leg of his journey by boat from Marseilles to Greece. The ship was Greek and typical of the new passenger boats which ploughed across the Mediterranean, and which were also used for cruises, a new and popular type of sea holiday for the British.

On a cruise one need never see the sea. Cruise ships had all the advantages of the Edwardian seaside pier: "First class accommodation boasts a ladies' room in dyed sycamore and pink brocade, a lounge in mahogany, a smoking room and a bar. The passengers were mainly Greeks, attired in the crest of fashion, and each endowed with sufficient clothes to last them without reappearance through the sixteen odd meals of the voyage. White trousers and mauve plusfours flashed above parti-coloured shoes ... jewels glittered; gowns clung; lips reddened; and all continued to ring the changes in face of increasing heat; while I lay about, cool and contemptible, in one shirt and a pair of trousers. Music was unceasing. Two pianos and a gramophone ministered to the 'fox trott' and 'Sharleston' ... The meals were served in the temperature of a blast furnace, stirred to its whitest by the vibrations of electric fans". When Robert Byron arrived he records that travel was by foot, boat and mule. There were few inns and those which existed were often unable to provide the simplest necessities demanded by the British visitors; three young men who were fortunately prepared for rough accommodation. "The host (of the inn at Caryes), moustached and collarless, accompanied by his two youthful assistants, conducted us by wooden ladder and wooden balcony to the upper floor. Sick of the company of one another we commanded three separate rooms, the two lesser at 1s. 3d. (6½p) a night, the larger an apartment of honour which was pressed upon us that it might not fall to the use of other and uncleanly visitors, at 2s. 6d. (12½p). The latter was decorated in the

Turkish fashion, with green plaster reliefs. Adjacent stood the bathroom, floored in lead and suspending from the ceiling a small watering can with an inverted funnel-mouthed·spout, which, when filled, would empty a seductive stream over the inviting back . . ."

"On descent, a lunch of macaroni, meat and French beans was placed before us. We sat at one of the numerous tables, on a bench. The whole ground floor was occupied by a low room, giving egress one side to the street and on the other to a kind of wooden staging hung with flowering creepers, and permitting through its cracks a view of unsavoury chickens. The meal finished, we demanded grapes. 'There are none' said the innkeeper". At which the English visitors casually took some from the garden. Afterwards, there were grapes available.

No harm came to Byron and his friends but there were still enough dangers in the Balkan countries to deter any visitors who were not adventurous. Civil wars had been a recent alarm and tales of wolves and bandits deterred most travellers. Bandits were not an empty threat, they roamed the mountains of Greece and parts of Southern Italy and would survive until our day in Sardinia. In many of the more remote parts of Europe the roads were still suitable for horses or mules but not for cars. If every village had a wine shop it did not follow that one could eat or sleep in it. Many areas were as they had been a hundred years before, and determined not to be disturbed by foreign visitors. Those who remember Italy, Greece or the Balkans before they were aware of their own value as tourist countries, say how unspoilt and beautiful they were. But many local people are probably relieved that the big 'buses bring them tourists from other parts of Europe. It had made them richer and some governments, delighted at the inrush of money from other countries, have ensured that beauty spots have proper drainage, decent roads and street lighting. These places may be less picturesque, but they are much more pleasant to live in.

And yet, unusual places were in demand in the 1930s, providing they had a decent hotel and good food! Max Rittenburg wrote a skit

Wintersports during the 1930s.

on holiday makers for *Punch*:

Travel Talk

(Overheard at Cook's)

Lady Violet de Parme (languidly to deferential assistant) "Yes, one really *must* go away somewhere at this time of year. What places have you got? . . . Riviera? Pau? Oh dear no! Much too banal. One meets all the people one knows at home . . . So *boring*. I want somewhere absolutely novel. Spain? Yes, that seems a little more interesting . . . Interpreter? Oh, of course they speak Spanish there, don't they?" She dismisses Spain. "Have you any other places? Sicily? Yes, Sicily might do . . . Italian isn't it, or is it French?

Thanks, I thought so. Would one have to eat Italian food, or could one get English food at the hotels? . . . Yes but I don't *care* to go to the overdone parts. I want somewhere absolutely novel . . . In the south of the island you say. Oh Sicily's an island is it? . . ."

After dismissing Sicily and Egypt, Lady Violet says: "Show me some places in the Desert. Sidi-Caique? Yes, Sidi-Caique sounds more tempting. Have they any decent golf links there? . . . Or an English doctor? . . . Any good motoring? . . . Yes I suppose the roads would be bad as you say, but if it's no use taking over our motor I don't know that I would *care* much about the Desert. Do you

4. ALEXANDRIE — Rosette Street

The package tour to Egypt usually included Alexandria.

think there would be any Bridge going? . . . Arn't there any fashionable people there this year, then? . . . Yes, I know quite well that I said I wanted somewhere right off the beaten track but I want a place where one can meet really nice people, and find golf and English cooking. *Surely* you understand what I am looking for? . . . yes, yes I suppose it *is* a little difficult to find these things together, but after all, your agency is for finding out those sort of places for us, *isn't* it? Then I suppose I shall have to stay in England after *all. Good* morning!''

The British demanded sport, plain food and each other's company and found those ingredients on their winter holidays even if they were unlucky in the summer. A few British visitors had made Switzerland popular in the nineteenth century. Then it had been admired for its scenery and cleanliness. By the 1920s it was beloved for its winter sports. The package deal holidays could rarely spread to St Moritz which was the expensive resort of the English, who arrived with skis and skates. At first skating was the great attraction but gradually skiing superseded it. Lots of jokes were made about broken arms and legs and many of them were based on unfortunate fact — winter sports could be dangerous and very tiring before ski lifts were installed which took the sportsmen up to the tops of the peaks down which they would glide. Many visitors enjoyed the social life of winter resorts as much as the skiing. The same society as that which had gathered about the Riviera a few months before, now congregated at St Moritz. Other winter sports resorts were established but none would achieve the same popularity with British visitors. Very few could enjoy winter holidays, especially when special equipment was needed for them. Winter sports would remain the exclusive pleasure of the rich until after the second world war when other resorts would open, even in other countries, for France and Italy suddenly realised that they had their share of mountains too.

It was bliss for the travel agencies in the 1930s. Package deals brought them customers who had never before had the chance to go abroad. Europe was opening up with new roads, new hotels, and faster, newer motor coaches, and all seemed to give impetus to the new craze. And while the mark, the franc and the lire remained low in price for the English it seemed as if the whole population could be walking in the Black Forest, sailing down the Rhine, paddling off the Riviera coast, or lying back in gondolas along the Grand Canal at Venice. Once seized by travel fever, most young British people expected to go abroad every year. Many of them went with the same groups each year and they would meet in January to decide where to go next. The pound sterling was worth so much that they felt they might travel anywhere and live cheaply and be welcome. It was a golden age of holidays abroad for the British.

Rien ne me résiste, tout me cède.
Er is niets dat mij weerstaat.
Everything gives way to me.

A joke post card from Normandy, 1930.

Fools' Paradise.

History books will tell you, quite rightly, that the second world war began in September 1939 but everybody in Britain was waiting for war the year before, rather like you wait for a thunderstorm. The air is heavy and your head aches, gradually clouds creep over the sky and a sultry overhot day is disturbed by a wind which suggests that thunder and lightning will follow. The year of 1938 was like that, full of suggestions of trouble to come.

It wasn't so easy for the comfortably off to ignore the unemployed who decided in 1938 that they would draw attention to themselves in a new way. They formed a National Unemployed Workers' Movement and organised Hunger Marches across Britain. In Oxford Street 200 unemployed men lay down in the road when the lights turned red, and dared the mass of traffic to cross over their bodies when they were green again. No car moved. Over their chests they held posters saying "Work or Bread". It was just before Christmas and the streets were crowded. Several hours later they slowly moved away.

It was not only the workers who were worried by the terrible lack of money, although they felt its problems more deeply than their ex-employers. It was typical of the time that the Cunard liners made cruises in the Mediterranean.

Their big liners were all imposing examples of British craftsmanship and rule over the waves. In the late 1920s the Cunard line had suffered a little from the Ile de France, the luxury liner launched from France which offered superb rooms (no old-fashioned cabins) and good food. Cunard also had enormous ships built between the wars, the Queen Mary and the Queen Elizabeth. These were intended for Trans-atlantic passages but as early as 1923 the big ships were seen as holiday resorts. They had enormous lounges filled with plants in tubs, dining rooms in which the white-clothed tables seemed to stretch for ever, swimming pools (for different classes of passengers), and often several dance bands. American Express (a large U.S. travel agency) hired the Mauritania in 1923 for a cruise of the Mediterranean. It was a completely new idea in holidays and almost immediately the steamship lines realised that rather than push their ships backwards and forwards from Southampton to New York, they could use some of them as floating hotels. Cunard had the Franconia built which was considered the most comfortable ship, and they "sold" the idea of travelling on it to millionaires. It was an extension of the thought that the very, very rich wish to be with their own kind on holiday, for it made them feel secure. What better way to ensure their ideal conditions for a holiday than to isolate them on a floating island? Besides, as Cunard cunningly pointed out, it was less expensive to cruise in a Cunard ship than to keep your own luxury yacht, on which you paid bills for upkeep and

View of the passengers in the restaurant of the Queen Mary, one of the most famous of the Cunard liners. (Radio Times Hulton Picture Library.)

staff all the year round. The Franconia was so much more grand than the most exclusive private ship! It had its own swimming pools, passengers could keep in touch with the stockmarket and buy and sell shares over the ship's radio, and there were lifts to carry you from one deck to another so that one did not have to exert oneself at all. The sales talk was so successful that Cunard reputedly "bagged" fifty millionaires for one cruise. Judge Gary, the head of a large American company, paid 25,000 dollars for a suite on

one cruise:– with a seat at the captain's table.

This "seat at the captain's table" had become a snobbish necessity for rich travellers. It was supposed to mean you were the most important people on board and film stars, business men and titled people all met up for dinner. There they would see who was important among the other passengers but also they would *be* seen by the envious guests who had to sit elsewhere. Some important people spoilt the custom by staying in their own cabins or suites for dinner which was

85

considered rather bad taste. The group at the captain's table were not only isolated among their own kind, but the people who saw them would say "I sailed with Mary Pickford or Anthony Eden or Amy Johnson on the Franconia, I saw them sitting at the captain's table". This easy identification of the "stars" on the trip gave everybody something to talk about and made those holiday-makers who wanted to see famous people travel on a Cunard cruise so that they could talk about their idols when they got home.

These ships did not seem to be at sea. They moved calmly across the ocean, stabilised by their great bulk. On them were cinemas, theatres, hairdressers, libraries, beauty parlours, bars of different kinds and comfortable rooms. Occasionally passengers might have a whiff of sea air if they went on deck but most of them did not travel to see the sea. They went on a cruise because it made them feel cosseted. The captain, who would have been a practical sailor a few years before, was more and more often chosen for his social graces. His crew actually saw to the sailing of the ship while he was pursued by his "guests". Many captains felt that they were degraded to being hotel managers.

By the late 1930s the big liners were almost a liability. They cost a great deal to run and had to be in operation all the time to make them worth keeping. The world cruises of the early 1930s were not wanted any more. Many of the rich who had been the best customers were suffering from the financial crashes in Wall Street and the City. Cunard started short cruises for a few weeks, in which the ships did not go very far, either round the Mediterranean where they looked like whales, or to the Canaries. It was a sign of hard times. In the coming war the big liners would be carrying troops and by 1945 some would be ready for the scrap heap. The short cruises were their swan song. Their panelled bars, their thickly carpeted passages, their chrome and stainless steel fittings, their long reclining deck chairs would be remembered with nostalgia as part of the style of the 1930s.

Cut price package deal holidays were still

the most popular way of going abroad for the new middle class: teachers, shop staff, clerks, or small businessmen who had not been hit by the Depression, flocked across the channel even while the murmurs of fear of Fascism were mounting. Perhaps in the foreboding of war to come many of them thought they should eat their cake while they could, for so many of these countries might alter if Hitler continued to march into them. And the mark and lire were so cheap! It seemed silly not to take advantage of what the travel agencies could offer. Agencies were beginning to explore further afield for lands for their clients. Dalmatia, Scandinavia, Holland and North Africa would have seemed too far or too unusual for holidays before but in the late 1930s they were added to the lists in the brochures which were so eagerly read in the winter months. If you couldn't afford to go abroad for very long you could always go on a day trip to the channel towns. The ferries took visitors to Boulogne, Calais, Ostend and Dieppe and for the first time it wasn't necessary to have a passport. There were alarmed mutterings about the new rule. Would criminals seize their chance to slip out of England? Or to come in when the boat unloaded at Dover on the return journey? But most of the travellers seemed to be curious Londoners "having a go" at a foreign country for the first time. The next adventure for the day tripper would probably be a whole week abroad booked through a travel agency.

A week's holiday was less of a fantasy for those workers who had work. For in 1937 the Amalgamated Engineering Union had arranged for its members to have two weeks holiday a year *with pay*. A fifth of the value of men's earnings was paid into a fund each week to finance their holidays.

Package deal holidays were so easy! All the anxious traveller had to do was travel to Victoria where he could identify his group by the badges worn by the couriers or holiday guides. Ushered onto the train, the holidaymakers found that the miraculously efficient courier took care of their luggage, escorted them on and off the boat and into a motor coach or onto a train when they were across the channel. The comfortable Briton didn't even have to know French, Italian or German, everything was taken care of, from finding lavatories to making sure that no "foreign muck" was served at dinner. And the "all in" price took care of everything: travel, hotel, meals and the service of the courier. Even tips were included in the cost ... £8 for cheap places, up to £14 or £15 for two weeks on the Riviera in a good middle class hotel. No wonder the British took advantage of those cheap years before the war, and the staff of hotels on the continent who had only seen the rich English before and had associated "British" with the old fashioned milords of the Edwardian age were shocked by the arrival of thirty or forty visitors who

carried straw bags and wore hats with artificial cherries on the bands, and dressed in frilly flowery dresses of artificial silk. However, they didn't stay shocked for long, for the new type of Briton on the continent was prepared to spend money on interminable cups of badly made tea, lemonade and sweets and to hire gondolas, bicycles, or the services of a local guide if their own courier was not available.

Even with such an easy opportunity to go abroad many English holiday-makers stayed at home. Often because of their children, but also because although holidays abroad were cheap if you travelled in a group, holidays in England were even less expensive. In 1937 you could get bed and breakfast in a boarding house at the seaside, during the summer season, for as little as 3s. (15p). A smarter

The Promenade, Cliftonville, Margate, 1937.

Victoria Terraces and Pier, Bridlington, 1936.

boarding house charged 7s. 6d. (37½p). These prices were recorded in Blackpool in the summer of 1937 by Mass Observers. The organisation of Mass Observation was founded by journalists and people with allied interests who wanted to find out what really made the British public tick. They investigated grim stories like the Munich crisis when the British Prime Minister went to reason with Hitler, but they also asked questions of the public about lighthearted things like the "Lambeth Walk" a popular dance of the time; or what people felt about wrestling and astrology. In the summer of 1937 they descended on Blackpool at the height of the summer season and wrote down what the holiday-makers felt about the town and their own impressions of it. It was an unfortunate choice in some ways because they had to sleep on benches on the beach. Seized by the same sort of hysteria as that of 1919 too many visitors had descended on Blackpool and there were no free rooms. However, the observers managed to make a

brave effort of recording what the town was like:

Bed and breakfast, as said above, was from 3s. to 7s. 6d. For full board, which meant a room with breakfast, midday meal and high tea at six o'clock, you would pay from 6s. to 9s. 6d. (30p – 47½p) in a boarding house. If you wanted to go up in the scale and chose a licensed hotel, you paid 15s. (75p) for full board. Those who had bed and breakfast picked up odd meals in the small cafés along the sea front, and for steak and chips they paid between 1s. 6d. and 2s. 6d. (7½p – 12½p). A cup of coffee was 4d. (1½p).

If you wanted entertainment Blackpool could offer you a most fascinating choice. Punch and Judy men still played on the sands, but the seafront promenade had enlarged until it stretched for the so-called Golden Mile. This was in fact 400 yards of joke shops, cafes, palmist's booths and amusement arcades. Every piece of land fronting on the sea was squeezed tight with little buildings, many of them very ricketty, each of which had its own attraction. Above these rather sordid booths soared the Blackpool Tower, built so many years before in imitation of the Eiffel Tower in Paris.

Two fortune tellers were reported by the Mass Observers. They had letters from royalty above their booths, which meant that they had displayed letters sent from Buckingham Palace thanking *them* for sending a letter, not that they had told the fortunes of the Royal Family. One of the most pathetic exhibits at Blackpool in 1937 was the Rector of Stiffkey; this unfortunate man had been defrocked (expelled) as a vicar and was sitting in a barrel fasting while curious crowds paid money to see him *not* eat. Next year the rector would move onto Skegness where he was eaten by lions when he extended his "act" to entering their cage.

The children had their own amusements in a separate area called the Pleasure Beach where the Noah's Ark was the chief attraction. This was an outsize model of the Noah's Ark with life size model animals set about it, as well as, mysteriously, a model policeman who flexed his knees. Going into the Noah's Ark was like going on a Ghost Train, the floor wobbled, hands seized you in the dark and blood-curdling cries broke the silence. It doesn't sound very suitable for children as the grown ups to whom the Mass Observers spoke had been quite frightened by it. The other important exhibit at Blackpool was Louis Tussaud's waxworks, a breakaway from the parent waxworks in London.

Mass Observation noticed that the shops were packed with models of the Tower which were eagerly bought, as well as Blackpool rock and white hats, rather like those worn by naval ratings but which had "Kiss me Quick" (the catchword of the time) and "Stop me" written round them. This all sounds very casual and racy but it's rather a surprise to find that in 1937 eight men out of ten wore a collar and tie, and in those days collars were usually stiff detachable ones which chafed the neck, so even if they went on the Cake walk at the Noah's Ark or stared at the Rector of Stiffkey or did the foxtrot in the Tower ballroom, the men who were on holiday were still quite formally dressed.

Some holidays at home were as well organised as those taken abroad. The early nudist camps had set the style for holiday

Cars come to the seaside, Swanage 1939.

camps which were a great success in the United States in the early 1930s and which were imitated in Britain. The first holiday camps were not at all like those we know today. They appealed to a completely different kind of customer, for they were serious attempts to bring together people with like interests and were used by fairly well-to-do, slightly intellectual visitors. They had themes such as musical holiday camps where string quartets played in the open air or Left Wing holiday camps in which lectures on politics were given. The organisers felt that only those who had specific reasons to get together would want to stay in these extensions of the old fashioned country house weekend for that was what they were like. The lecturers or performers would stay in a large country house into which would be packed as many guests as possible and the overflow would stay in extensions of the house which were either prefabricated cabins or tents. Most of the guests liked the informality of eating together and there was still a strong minority of those who were vegetarian and who enjoyed the specialised canteen food which was served. As a prime reason for the holiday was talking, the notion of cabins

The holiday camp in 1939. (Radio Times Hulton Picture Library.)

set in large grounds became popular for several guests could meet to discuss the concerts or lectures. It was extraordinary that the guests enjoyed the communal spirit and willingly went on rambles together. They also seemed to enjoy gymnastics and Keep Fit classes which were run by the camp.

It was not surprising that more commercially minded holiday caterers thought that these holiday camps might be a good idea for the general public. It was very courageous of them to start camps, for so far only more eccentric people had shown any interest in them. Would holiday camps be popular if they didn't have a theme, like the musical camps for serious visitors? Would the average holiday-maker appreciate the necessary regimentation that was the rule in a holiday camp? In a boarding house guests could have as much or as little to do with each other as they liked, but in a holiday camp they must enjoy the company of other people. One great attraction of the holiday camp was its suitability for children. Boarding houses and hotels did not always welcome them and most people couldn't afford to rent country cottages. Besides it was

the middle class mother who was prepared to spend her whole holiday cooking and amusing their children. Most women who had more strenuous everyday lives wanted to escape from their children but couldn't. By providing babysitters and children's amusements the holiday camps could be successful.

Funfair proprietors opened some of the early camps because they saw how important organised amusements were going to be in a family holiday. Many camps were sited near funfairs or by the sea so that there was a continual source of pleasure. The camp owners built wooden huts in groups round the communal dining room and games rooms. They set out to appeal to the less well paid white collar workers: — shop assistants, clerks and commercial travellers. Once in the camp the visitors had everything provided for them . . . meals, entertainment and swimming pools. Billy Butlin opened one of the first camps at Skegness in 1937; by 1939 there were a hundred holiday camps.

1937 and 1938 were years when everybody was conscious of the healthy outdoor life and keeping fit. Playing fields were being opened

CHILDRENS YACHTING POND, PEASHOLM, SCARBOROUGH.

A beauty competition at Butlins in 1939. (Radio Times Hulton Picture Library.)

in memory of the late King George V. There was immense interest in sports in which the public could participate. While the middle classes puffed over newly made golf courses, the younger and poorer men went cycling and swimming or joined small local football teams. While they managed their own kind of "keep fit" their wives earnestly slimmed, for slimming was a fad which was not to disappear like so many crazes of the 1930s.

Imagine the summer of 1939. War has been in the air for so long that many would-be holiday-makers don't believe it will ever come. Children have been fitted for gas masks, emergency plans have been made to evacuate schools to the country from the towns if air raids seem probable. But the nation decides to "chance" a holiday. For many people the last holiday before the war would remain an exquisite memory to carry for six years.

"Good breakfasts" says one writer remembering a private seaside hotel: "eaten in a silence broken only by the clearing of throats . . . the hasty scamper across the promenade, raincoats tightly buttoned over long one-piece bathing suits for it was not 'done' to change on the beach . . . endless cups of morning coffee, the careful choice of coloured postcards".[1]

In a hundred Bella Vistas and Mon Abris the bacon is liberally served at breakfast and butter slapped on fresh rolls. Rationing will make these holiday breakfasts seem like feasts. Landladies purse their lips as children trail sandy buckets across their lino-covered hall floors. Damp bathing suits are surreptitiously dried in the bedrooms by electric fires fed by penny-in-the-slot meters. Longer skirts are back and the visiting ladies swish about the promenade with some of the elegance of those Edwardians who came into the beginning of our story, but they have expressions and behaviour the Edwardians would not have recognised. They exclaim "ripping" and "frightful" and occasionally a more self-assured mother will look to see that none of her children can hear her before she

275. LE HAVRE — Sur la plage à l'heure du bain

Le Havre: plenty of activity.

The Sands, Westcliff on Sea.

On the beach in 1911.

Pleasure Steamer leaving the Pier Eastbourne 3342.

Pleasure Steamer 1920.

mutters a "bloody" ... which is thought a very upper class word and is drawn out behind a long cigarette holder. Fathers scan the *Daily Mail* for news of the possibility of war, see none, and retire to deck chairs where they cover their faces with the newspaper for one of those snoozes which take up so much time on their holidays. Similar scenes are played out opposite them, on the other side of the channel where many of the holiday makers are also English. They are dripping in the sea at Dieppe and Dinard, those sandy resorts which are so suitable for children who dig furiously on the beaches where a short time later the Germans will also be digging in foundations for gun turrets, and planting barbed wire and mines. France in the August and September of 1939 seems so idyllic. In the more fashionable resorts of Deauville and Le Touquet the English drink cocktails on the terraces of hotels overlooking the sea, and think about betting on the races which attract them to Normandy. These resorts are easily accessible to them owing to the airfield at Le Touquet.

Perhaps after lunch they will take a few francs and go and have a flutter in the casino. They might win a little extra towards the cost of their holiday!

Few of them know or would believe that an arrangement has been made between the French and British governments to ensure that enough petrol will be available to drive these British holiday makers back to the coast when they take flight for the cross channel ferries. It is Saturday, September 2nd; fine weather, and sailing boats off the coasts of Normandy and Brittany can be easily seen dipping their red and white sails as they flutter round each other like butterflies. It is so clear that the English can see their own coastline rising out of the sea, its white cliffs deceptively innocent in the calm blue light. Some of them will have their wirelesses on when Chamberlain speaks on the following morning, an equally warm and calm Sunday, and, suddenly afraid, they will run towards their beloved baby cars, or towards those couriers who will have the thankless task of shepherding alarmed holidaymakers out of the continent and back to the safety of England.

Even in their fear most of them would not believe that it will be at least six years before they take a holiday abroad and that when they next set foot in France, Italy or Germany it will be as servicemen, not as tourists sucking ice-creams and posing for "snaps" by the local ruins. Many of the places they visit will never be the same again — but then neither will the visitors.

1. Richard Collier: *A House called Memory.* Collins 1960.

As our grandparents were in 1901.

95

Acknowledgments

The author wishes to thank the following for their help in supplying photographs for this book.

Glasgow Evening Times. p 16.
University of Leeds, Department of Folk Life and Dialect Studies. pp 19, 23 and 60.
The Radio Times Hulton Picture Library. pp 13, 34, 53, 60, 69, 70, 78, 85, 90 and 92.
The Scott Macfie Collection by courtesy of the Librarian, Liverpool University Library. pp 50 and 51.
The Scout Association. p 61.
Mr. Leslie Bainbridge, Editor of Health and Efficiency. p 72.
Scarborough Public Library. p 38.

Also for permission to quote from the following publications.

The Edwardian Story: Desmond Shaw. (Rockcliff 1949.)
My Autobiography: Charles Chaplin. (Bodley Head 1964.)
Ask the fellows who cut the hay: George Ewart Evans. (Faber 1956.)
Miss Clare Remembers: "Miss Read". (Michael Joseph 1962.)
The Country Child: Alison Uttley. (Faber 1931.)
"Low Tide" from the Collected Stories of Osbert Sitwell. (Macmillan 1953.)
Laughter in the next room: Osbert Sitwell. (Macmillan 1949.)
A Clergyman's Daughter: George Orwell. (Gollancz 1935.)
The Station: Robert Byron. (John Lehmann 1949.)
A House called Memory: Richard Collier. (Collins 1960.)
Mr. Punch and his Travels: (Max Rittenberg 1932.)